MDC
Al Schvitz:
Double Life in Double Time

Stories of Punk, Prison & Perseverance

Alan "Al Schvitz" Schultz

Manic D Press
San Francisco

MDC Al Schvitz: Double Life in Double Time ©2018 Alan Schultz. Published by Manic D Press. All rights reserved.   ISBN 978-1-945665-07-3
For information, please address Manic D Press, PO Box 410804, San Francisco, California 94141   www.manicdpress.com   Printed in Canada

This book was written quite a long time ago, when I had some time on my hands. It isn't unusual to write such a book while in jail, and this story hasn't had much overhauling.

MDC still has two of its original members, me and singer Dave Dictor. Mikey "Offender" Donaldson and Frank "Franco" Mares have both passed. Mikey was the youngest band member we ever had, and Franco was a sprout-loving, spirulina-eating, vegetarian health nut. That I, the oldest in the band and a hard-partying cigarette smoker, outlived these guys is in itself amazing.

MDC is, at present, still putting out albums and touring. Forty-five years of friendship with singer Dave Dictor and almost forty years of band history will do that sometimes, if one is very lucky. And this I have been.

Forty years is long time. So what is here is what I originally wrote without changing it to make me look any wiser than I was back then. Please take my word that I've learned a few things since this was written. We all are changed by time and the events we live through.

Alan "Al Schvitz" Schultz

"Well...," an awkward word to begin my lament, I know, but I ask you to be patient with me as this is my first day on the job. (Experience helpful, but not necessary.) They say patience is a virtue. I've learned a bit about patience.

After all, I am but a drummer, which means I only learned to count to four anyway. I know, I know, you're thinking "what about 5/4 time, or 7/8 time?" True, these time signatures do have beyond four, but a true drummer will count it "1-2-3-4, 1-2-3," or "1-2, 1-2, 1-2-3," or some other way of reducing it to a drummer's common denominator.

At any rate, I don't mean "Well..." as much as I probably mean "Why?" and more particularly, "Why now?" That question has mostly to do with my present address: Alan Schultz, Prisoner #1561776, County Jail #3 at San Bruno, P.O. Box 6794066, San Bruno, California.

While I would prefer to be able to say that I was here doing research for Sociology 101, or that I was a political prisoner, I'm in jail for selling drugs. I would also like to be able to say that I was a victim of circumstances and totally innocent of all charges but as my good friend and attorney, Chip, would tell you, I was one of the best he had ever seen at the two professions I practiced: playing drums, and selling drugs and making money at it. So, back to the "Why now?" The "now" is April 20, 1995, and the "why" is between here and San Quentin, my probable destination. (The thought of which scares the hell out of me.) I seem to have an abundance of, yes, TIME.

I find myself in a position in Punk Rock few people have enjoyed, as somewhat of a sacred cow with icon status. This, coupled with my very fair (and even generous) business practices, held me in good stead and allowed me a great deal of success. I thought that no one would roll over on me, that is, snitch me out. With all of the cut-the-drugs, Epsom-selling, rip-offs on the street, fronting themselves off like sunken-cheeked neon signs, and spreading their heat like cheap margarine in every doorway in the Tenderloin (San Francisco's Skid Row), why would anyone want to fuck me over? Many people considered me to be the best meth dealer in town. I've lived in San Francisco for twelve years and can tell you unequivocally that no dealer ever treated me nearly as well as I treated people. So I operated naively for about three years, making thousands, and giving away the store.

As it turns out, someone did "confidentially inform." The cops busted in and caught me with a sizable amount of speed (four or five ounces of glass, beautiful stuff that I had made specially for a particular client of mine to be shipped to the East Coast), $5500 or so dollars, which turned into $3300 by the time it got down to police headquarters (will wonders never cease?), the bags, the scale (digital, Tinita model 1479, the industry's standard, of course), and everything but OJ Simpson's glove. Though one would think by the way the cops gloated that they had found OJ's glove, Jimmy Hoffa's cufflinks, and a rattle from the Lindbergh baby. I'll never learn the identity of the rat because I'm planning to take the deal for sixteen months in the state pen, most likely San Quentin. This will probably return me to the world the soonest.

This is sooner or later going to be a book about music, travel, politics (both personal and beyond), and starkly contrasted ups and downs. And mostly, a book about friends and friendship. Be patient, Dear Reader, for — as I'm finding out the hard way — patience is a virtue, and I can be about as virtuous as they make me.

Another reason I shoved off on this literary voyage is my last court appearance. I was guilty as sin and, due to my past transgressions, facing some serious jail time. A prison stretch, in fact. To try and avoid this unpleasantness, my best friend was going to fall on the sword of dope for me. His record was clean but this would certainly dirty it up some and could land him some suspended jail time.

As I walked into the courtroom and saw his corny new haircut, big smile, and silly-looking skinny uncoordinated necktie, I knew I couldn't go through with it. This was not what I was made of and certainly not the act of a friend. This selfless man was and is Dave Dictor. For better or worse, nobody would change my life for the next two decades as much as he.

Well, these gangsterly, cranksterly events have led me to this point. At the risk of being unoriginal, I think this story is best told in flashback. I won't claim to have been there in Punk Rock from the very start because in 1978 I was working in real estate in New York City. However, this tale — saga? story? I'll know better what to call it when I'm finished — of Millions of Dead Cops begins in 1973.

I can foresee now that this book is going to be laced with truths, most of which I had to find out for myself to be true. One of these is that at age eighteen one knows absolutely everything, or at least everything of any real importance. As one grows up, we learn just how little we really do know, and how naive and narrow our worldly little eighteen-year-old viewpoint was.

I was a lousy student in high school. At the time, I was certain that I would only be playing drums for a living. I was a bit advanced for my age, for I knew everything there was to know at age seventeen! School seemed an unimportant second to the "being cool" that was a prerequisite to my future profession. Funny thing is, had I been a good student, I never would have met Dave Dictor in Tampa, Florida. I was there attending an accept-anyone-who-has-the-tuition college, the University of Tampa.

Being from Long Island and New York City, I considered myself kind of a post-Woodstock, post-Vietnam War, hippie New Yorker in a world of free-thinking Americans who had all lived through the same Vietnam War-hating, music and peace love-dove, long-haired experience that I had. Didn't everyone watch TV? Didn't everybody see the fall of Richard Nixon and the rise of the Grateful Dead? Didn't everybody worship Jethro Tull in theaters like the Fillmore East and Howard Stein's Mateus at the Palladium? And hadn't everyone committed to memory the Jefferson Airplane's *Volunteers*? "Look what's happening out in the street… One generation got old… one generation got soul… but this generation got no destination to hold… Pick up the cry!"

To my chagrin, some folks — in fact, a whole big chunk of the USA — were rednecks proud to be American, short haired, love-it-or-leave-it, football star worshipping throwbacks to the Stone Age, that is, the 1950s, and it seemed that most of these post-WWII idiots lived in and around Tampa.

I was in a dorm called Delo Hall, and found out that I had jock roommates. I don't remember their names because the third time they told to turn down The Band's live double-album *Rock of Ages*, I'd had it. In my meanderings around the dorm I came to Room 309, where a large space was unoccupied. So, stereo and Dead tapes, Procol Harum and Pink Floyd records in hand, I was warmly welcomed by one Scott Gilbert and one David Scott Dictor. This day in September 1973, Al Schvitz, as I came to be known, met Dave MDC. It would be some eight years later, and two thousand miles away, that a serious musical venture would arise in (of all places) Austin, Texas.

Basically, I believe that had it not been for my continued friendship with my singer Dave — having existed and grown for years before — that a band such as ours could have enjoyed the longevity it has, despite the financial success it hasn't.

So, Dear Reader, if your reason for reading this is an interest in the anatomy of a rock band — a self-made musical organization that has sold out culture palaces in Moscow, played more than nine hundred shows in over thirty countries, started a record label that helped launch bands like DRI (to whom I shamefully acknowledge still owing money) and a compilation with 55 bands from all over the world (a mixing and mastering nightmare, I assure you!), and managed to keep itself together for fifteen years (no small accomplishment!) — you will have to put up with a little more history.

Let me return to 1973. Dave and I came from towns about ten miles apart on Long Island, and from similarly liberal backgrounds. This led to our having similar outlooks on life. The town I'm from is Great Neck, the closest town outside of New York City's borough of Queens. I could see the Empire State Building from the house I lived in until I was 15 years old. In truth, I had to climb a tree to see it, which I did often.

Our shared point-of-view had at its center, I'm happy to say, music. Of course, the center of our world was the center of the universe (being eighteen and all). The other center to our little world was the ever-entrancing, enticing, and alluring world of illicit drugs. Some people experimented with drugs. We were into out and out research!

This subject being no small part of my history, it is probably germane to the story to go back to where, when, and who was involved in my separating from the normal kid that my parents would have ideally wished me to have been to the eventual criminal that landed in jail and then prison, for gosh sakes.

Funny, but sometimes it seems that time and events blur. I don't mean that I don't remember them; I do, with surprising vividness. I mean, as I look back, it seems that time and events almost had a will of their own, like a roller coaster that gains momentum. I am not saying that I was caught in a vicious cycle, poor friggin' me. No, I knew smoking pot was bad in eighth grade, and that few of my eighth-grade peers were doing it. But it was just one of those things that was enticing. The people who were smoking were older, hipper types whom I had met by going to New York City when I was old enough to catch the Long Island Railroad to Penn Station, when I was about thirteen years of age.

I would go to a concert at the Fillmore East with my friends; we were old enough to jump on the train to the City and take a subway. I loved the music and the hippies and, although I thought that the Vietnam War would be long over before I had anything to fear from the draft, I hated war and loved the idea of protesting the government, and all that stuff that I should not have been embracing for another five to eight years. And I loved my long hair. This was all fitting in with fact that I fully intended to be a musician as I said, and, well, drugs were a little more of the smoke and mirrors that were the bows and ribbons or magic that made the whole rock and roll lifestyle irresistible to a thirteen-year-old from Long Island. This was the beginning of "the seduction" as I later referred to those times, and the bad choices I wasn't really aware that I was making.

My parents never used drugs and they believed way back then that marijuana was the same as, or at least could lead to, the hard stuff. I am so glad that my dad never found out what I was into before he passed. However, his passing eliminated the next hurdle that my roller coaster faced in creeping up to the top where... *Wheee!* Hands in the air!

The summer I turned 16 was a big summer for taking acid, barrels of orange sunshine, 1969. I never had a bad trip but a few friends of mine did, including one who ran through a plate-glass door. I lost my fascination for it but it was okay for its time. I outgrew it, I guess, and it no longer appealed to me.

One time at a party, around when I was 17, this beautiful blonde-haired girl, older than me, came out of the bathroom looking for someone to tie up her arm. At the time I remember thinking I'd like to try that some time. That was in NYC; it was heroin. Tried it, didn't like it.

Let me be clear, at no time was I glad my father wasn't around. Nor do I believe that he would have been able to do much more than slow my decline (if you want to call it that). I couldn't have been more fortunate with parents. My folks were gentle, well-educated, financially comfortable. I never heard my parents fight. My dad adored my mom, who was vivacious, blond, and 12 years his junior. My dad was a lawyer, and did very well for himself and his little family. Yes, I was an only child, and it was September 8, 1954, the day I was born in

Doctors Hospital on the fashionable Upper East Side of Manhattan. By the time I was aware, JFK's Camelot was in full swing. The nation had never before known such abundance, nor has it since… Doesn't sound like a breeding ground for a drug lord to me.

But there was a situation brewing in the international front by the time I was in my teens. A "police action," they called it. My father was the first person I ever heard say that we shouldn't get involved in Vietnam. He said it to one of his friends over dinner one night. These people, my parents and their friends, were older folks. My dad was born in 1907. They were all college grads and much smarter than me. I remember my dad saying that those Asian people were poor and that communism was a reasonable way of dealing with the lack of basic commodities that the Third World countries suffered with (or something to that effect).

When his friend expressed a differing point of view, my dad — this I remember exactly though decades have passed since he said it — said, "Oh, come on, you don't believe that ridiculous 'domino theory' stuff, do you? Do you really think that the Vietnamese are going to sail across the Pacific to San Francisco and take over?" They all laughed at the absurdity of my dad's remark.

Meanwhile, I'm thinking, "This is what they are teaching me in school during current events." I couldn't wait until I heard my teacher use that domino rubbish again. I didn't have to wait long. Within a day or so, the "police action" was back in the news and my teacher was back to the old standard over-simplification explanation for us 13-year-olds. Off I went, waving my hand like it was raining and my teacher was the last taxi in Manhattan. I couldn't be ignored. When poor unsuspecting Miss Tarbell said, "Yes, Alan, you have a question?"

I replied, "Yes, ma'am, I'm not sure I understand this theory. Are you seriously saying that if we don't stop these poor hungry Asians by shooting up their country, that at some point they are going to get up from their rice paddies and sail over here to attack San Francisco or something?" My comment wasn't as clever to my teacher and the principal as my dad's was to his friends.

I know, I appear to be rambling but my point is that even though my dad and I shared the same view on the Vietnam War, his dying just before my fifteenth birthday, allowed me to be swept into adulthood unfettered by any serious discipline thereafter. All of a sudden I was attending only the late shows at the Fillmore, which occasionally wouldn't end until it was light outside. We would come out, wincing in the morning light, taking the subway to the train, and I'd stumble in my front door about 8 or 9 a.m., something that certainly would not be happening if my dad was still alive.

My father was a really good man, and my life might have been different if he hadn't passed from heart problems at the age of 62, when I was not yet 16. My mom was his second wife; he had a couple of kids from his first marriage, but we didn't have any contact. A few years ago, one of my much older half-brothers came to an MDC gig in Florida and had a great time. He was going to stay for a few songs but stayed the whole gig.

"I had no idea!" he told me. "I loved it!" which was the closest I have ever come to approval for my Punk Rock career from my dad, and it meant a lot to me and still does. So, anyway, back to the events circa 1973ish in Tampa.

What was unusual about us was our backwards surroundings. Dave and I had visited other colleges, but this place was ancient, like ten or more years behind the times. I did get to know Freddy Solomon, the football player, and even shared a bag of pot with him, but associations like that were few. Funny how he also gravitated to San Francisco and played for the 49ers. Pro football player John Matuszak was also in our dorm, but he was an obnoxious asshole. Matuszak would, for example, get on the only elevator and not let anyone push their floors until he got to his. A real charmer.

"What has this to do with rock and roll?" you may well ask. I didn't say I had the answer. Still, I'm going to relate some things that happened to Dave and me back in Tampa, back in the beginning.

Delo Hall was the men's dorm, and Dave and I thought this to be ridiculous. Being the co-ed dorm, *Harrad Experiment* age, this needed changing, so we made an appointment with Dean West, the dean of housing. We had our rap down. This separation was unhealthy and unnatural. It was producing sexually stifled, frustrated people. This was not preparing for healthy relationships in the future. This tyranny needed abolition, and the co-ed dorm freedoms of the colleges of the North should be the replacement. Well, Dean West listened with remarkable patience considering that he was a Southerner and, as I discovered scanning his office wall, was also a Baptist minister and head of the Theology department, not to mention that his father was a founder of this very private, very Southern little college.

As the whole picture was settling in on me, I can hear Dave admirably going on and on about the state of the dorm situation, knowing full well he hasn't realized what I've discovered. I nudged Dave, directing his attention to the documents I'd just perused, and listened to his speech kind of wind down as he figured out what my hesitation was about. We thanked Reverend West kindly for his time and hightailed it out of his office on the verge of busting out laughing. Needless to say, the dorms remained as they had before and probably will as long as the sky is blue.

Then, there was Gasparilla Day. Supposedly — I've never cared enough to check it out — José Gaspar, the pirate, discovered Tampa as a stash for all his plunder. Gaspar was a celebrated pirate, who was probably half as rich and twice as bloodthirsty as the legend claims. At any rate, to commemorate his vicious crime spree and his wonderful discovery — namely Tampa, Florida USA — a holiday, complete with parade, was an annual event. The coolest thing about this yearly ritual was the replica of Gaspar's ship, The Gasparilla! It was as close to the actual article as one could find, and it even sported the original bow maiden from the real Gasparilla. This was enough for me to crave its pirate flag. Only one day and one night would the ship have flags: the night before and the day of the parade.

Dave and I decided we were going to try and steal the pirate flag. By the way, I forgot to mention that whoever decides these things was thoughtful enough to dock The Gasparilla right across the river from our school! So much for "out of sight, out of mind." And who was more out of their minds than Dave and me? Truth be told, it was mostly my obsession.

We set out that night in black, looking like characters out of Belushi's *Animal House*. We were sneaking around like it was Faber College and we were avoiding Dean Wormer. Ironically, the University of Tampa in '73 was frighteningly similar to that Animal House college, circa 1962: the alumni bought cars for the football players, and the players and cheerleaders pranced around like French poodles. Unfortunately, the only way to get that pirate flag was to climb the mizzenmast to the top. Then climb boot-camp style over across the steel cable to the main mast, drop into the crow's nest, and detach the flag from there. Oh, to be young and stupid again!

I made the climb up the mizzenmast, which resulted in friction burns on my thighs for weeks. Then I tore chunks out of my T-shirt, wrapped my hands, and started across the steel tightrope, which arched its way to the top of the ship. I was halfway there when I realized I didn't think I could make it. Had it been closer to go back than ahead, I'd probably have done just that, but as fate would have it, forward or back were about the same distance, and my main direction of concern at the time was down! I now understood the extent of my commitment to this little venture. So, in great fear, I pressed on. I had flipped over and was hanging by my hands and legs under the cable. From there I inch-wormed toward the crow's nest. I reached out when I was near enough and grabbed the edge. I slowly and awkwardly nudged myself over the rim, and dropped head first — or should I say face first? — safely into the nest. I turned over on my back and caught my breath. All right, it's easy from here: throw down the flag to Dave, rewrap my hands, slide down to the mizzenmast, down to the deck, and we're home free. A snap!

"You up there, Al?" I heard Dave call. I started laughing incredulously. Where else could I be?

"No one here but us chickens!" I replied and continued laughing.

I was totally out of breath from the climb. I was a pack-a-day smoker, and even at eighteen it had taken its toll, and the laughter had made me light-headed, as well as weak. I struggled to my knees, and peered over the edge of the crow's nest.

Holy shit! It seemed like miles to the deck! Did I say "a snap"? Did I think "home free"? All I could think now was that I wished I had stayed home and studied for the American Studies exam I would ultimately fail the next day. And that's when the cops showed up.

Oh, fuck! on top of Holy Shit! Four cop cars pulled up from two directions. The Gasparilla was "being stolen" or "under siege" or whatever they call it when one (Dave was long gone by then) skinny little college freshman is hiding in the crow's nest of a ship docked in a river. The police were shining lights and bullhorning up at me. I hid under Roger, as the pirate flag eventually came to be known. Not too original, but it fits. I lay there and didn't move a muscle.

"Well, no one is going to climb up there," I heard one of the cops say. "You'd have to be some kind of an idiot!" He was right. Eventually they left but I thought they were waiting for me so I stayed up there for what seemed like hours, thinking, "Well, if they jump out during my escape, I'll jump in the river and swim for the school." I'd already tied Roger around my neck and hands. Much to my relief, the cops really were gone. I used Roger to slide down to the mizzenmast, down to the deck, and scampered home. Not as romantic as swimming the river but at least the flag was mine.

When I got Roger home to my dorm room, we spread him out and discovered that it was a 9' x 12' piece of canvas sail material. Did I say "swim"? With Roger tied around my neck and hands, I would have been the deadest drowned bilge rat ever to be washed out to sea! Thank you, Tampa PD, for your underestimation of one kid's headstrong stupidity. We didn't know it then, but Roger was to be MDC's backdrop for our first tours, and would reside in The Fuck Ups' storefront window when not on tour. The Fuck Ups were a local San Francisco punk band, perhaps *the* local punk, in the Mission neighborhood in 1980.

I can see that time and space are going warp back and forth in this as I want to jump up to 1980 and talk about The Fuck Ups, Verbal Abuse, Code of Honor, Sick Pleasure, and a dozen others, but I am going to restrain myself chronologically once again and not jump. After writing down this tale of our young selves, I decided to give Dave a call and tell him what I had written. He reminded me of another story significant to the birth of MDC. This, however, is not a tale of fun or pranks. This is a story of the death of a friend.

Some of MDC's songs were written way before there was an MDC to play them. Well, maybe not the song itself, but the events and inspirations that certainly influenced our songbook. "I Remember" was one of those songs. It was inspired by, and dedicated to, the memory of Tate Bryan.

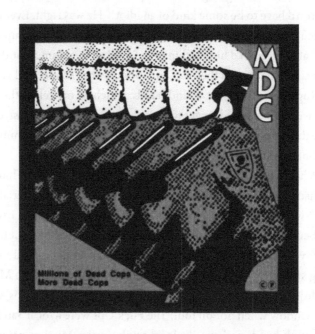

2

Tate Bryan and his friend from childhood, Steve, had come to Tampa together from St. Louis. They each had a motorcycle, and so did I. We became pals, and did a lot of riding and drugs together, mostly Dilaudids, Demerols, and the like.

One night, Steve and I decided to do this drugstore. We had cased it for days, never really planning to pull it off. But, on this night, Steve told me that he had been going inside and checking it out as far as alarms and cameras were concerned. He also had made mental notes as to where the choice loot was to be found. Hypothetically speaking, of course.

So, armed with this new information, Steve and I borrowed a car, and proceeded to Nebraska Avenue between Fletcher and Fowler Streets in North Tampa. Why Tate wasn't with us, I don't recall. This store was ideally located between streets, and only approachable from a ways off. This provided adequate time to get away into a wooded area at the first sign of trouble. A real piece of cake. We got away with a pillowcase full of pill bottles. Demerols, Dilaudids, Dilaudid cough syrup, Dilaudid suppositories, Seconals, Nembutals, and a whole lot of useless stuff. One doesn't take time to sort out one's acquisitions during a heist. Plenty of time to do that back home. Tate, having seen our haul, decided without telling anyone to do his own store the very next night.

The store he chose was not a piece-of-cake, however. He broke into a pharmacy in a mall. The police were alerted by a silent alarm.

The account I'm about to give is what filtered through an investigation, and is as I recall after twenty years' time. Death being the sort of thing that tends to date one's life. I know it's the truth when I realize that my friend and biking buddy died over twenty years ago. Most things fall into a certain proportion with time. Time does heal all wounds. One shouldn't forget, however, that some wounds heal leaving deep scars, scars that can be seen by others, and some so deep that they can only be seen within. Yes, it's twenty years hence but these events I remember as if they occurred yesterday.

I found out about Tate from the morning newspaper. A picture of Tate on the front page told of his burglary attempt, and made it sound pretty cut and dried. What was later discovered was that the silent alarm turned on a video and audio tape recorder. This tape revealed the horrible truth.

The police had pulled up, and Tate had taken off running into an adjacent field. The tape revealed that the officer hadn't shouted, "Stop or I'll shoot!" Neither had the warning shot the pig claimed to have fired been recorded.

This fucking "hero" cop took a hunting rifle, complete with scope, from his own arsenal, and executed Tate, who was unarmed and running away through a field. Shot dead, without warning, at age eighteen. The butcher that shot Tate in the back, unarmed, got a two-week suspension …or should I say more accurately, vacation with pay. This animal returned to work in two weeks and a day after satisfying the department's internal cover-up inquiry.

One lone shot had been fired. No warning, either shouted or fired. And the result was the whole right side of Tate's chest was blown out. The coroner said he was dead before he hit the ground. Listening to the tape when it was turned up, one could hear the faint whistle or whine that was the sound of Tate's final breath escaping from his left lung through the hole in his right.

Some said a lot more trouble would have been stirred up if Tate had been a local. As it was, his parents were in no shape to do anything but come claim Tate's possessions and head back to St. Louis to bury their son.

Meanwhile, unaware of Tate's death, Steve had decided to leave town right away. He was feeling nervous, and now had enough cash to make the trip. Steve took off riding his 850 Commando Norton motorcycle. He got home and his girlfriend had decided to break up with him. When Steve heard about Tate, it was too much. He took his own life with a handgun.

Steve had left an Aria hollow-body electric guitar I later sold to Dave. I hadn't learned to play yet. It was surely a guitar made to play the blues.

The shock and horror of these events wore away to leave a hollow empty hole in my heart for my fallen friends, and a resentment of the police that I will take to my grave. DEAD COPS, Millions of DEAD COPS!!! It's at least a good start!

I began to think about cops more and more. Dave's brother, Roger, was a cop. He used to say there were three kinds of cops: one kind joined the force out of a genuine concern for protecting people from bad guys. Roger was that type, and a really sweet guy who had saved babies from open window ledges when their addict moms were nodded out, and stuff like that. Roger is my favorite of Dave's six brothers. He hurt his back lifting a manhole cover on the job.

The second type of cop was the authoritarian bully. They usually played football in high school. I know it seems like I have a problem with football players. I really don't. Dave even used to play in high school, but he was kicked off the team for smoking pot. Right on, Dave! Anyway, the second was a bully who loved forcing authority down people's throats, sometimes with a billy club. They swagger around like John Wayne, "Playing cops for real, playing cops for pay!" as Jello Biafra would say. The sort that got a real kick out of arresting old black winos and beating them up while laughing about how they made those bums piss themselves. The Chicago Democratic National Convention, Rodney King-bludgeoning type of chickenshit "hero" that probably abuses his family at home every night.

Then there's the third kind: the sort of wishy-washy, gutless wonder that leans the way of convenience. Some of these had grown mellow from the second kind, and others had grown callous from the first kind, or just let the vibes get to them. After all, LAPD, for example, armed and dressed in stormtrooper uniforms, including handcuffs, clubs, mace, .38 caliber revolver or similar handgun, a belt containing dozens of extra rounds, shotgun in the car, breastplates, and other accoutrements. This life-or-death outfit breeds fear and resentment, especially from minorities. These constant vibes of hate and "power of life and death in my hand" results in turning a well-meaning cop into a bully-type cop. Now, right or wrong is one thing, but nowadays I find myself not thinking right and wrong, or of crime and punishment. I think of safe and unsafe.

The bottom-line effect is all around me, here in jail. The great majority of inmates are black or Latino. Fortunately, I learned early in the jail game, especially in the Bay Area, when the cops ask if you're gay, say "Yes." That way you'll be in with many more white guys busted for drugs. It's much better than being thrown in with a group of people of color who think your lily-white ass is just a little too much like the cop who busted them, the judge who sentenced them, and the jailers and sheriffs who locked the cage in which you now reside with them. Anyway, I'm getting away from myself again.

It's Friday night, here in jail, and I'm hoping for a visit from my kids, Brian and Marie. But I know finding someone who has a car, a license for ID necessary to get in, no criminal record (which they do check), and being responsible enough for their mother and me to trust with our kids is a few-and-far-between sort of thing, so I'm not expecting any miracles. Jail's just like that.

Yesterday started off good. They let us out in the yard for the first time in nineteen days. Imagine not being off that jail tier for almost three weeks. It's crazy.

Then the day turned into evening. The jail actually had musical instruments donated by some church for the inmates. It was their version of music theory class: this clown thumped the Bible at us for almost an hour. He then played his corny choir's demo tape.

Christ! I thought. I spoke up, and started accusing Jesus of causing more blood to spill than Hitler, and made a good case for not believing at all. Then, as I expected, when I got to the subject of Northern Ireland, he kicked me out. Now there's the power of Jesus for you. I thought I wanted to play some music. I knew I wanted to play! But to wade through that much bullshit was more than I could bear. I really have too much respect for myself and too much love for music. They tested me for drugs on the way back to the tier. Speaking of which, I'd been expecting a very special "spiced" letter to come, and it hasn't. It's three or four days late, and I fear I'll never get it now. So, that's a day in the life at good old County Jail #3 in San Bruno, California. I was attending a few classes. The only one I think worth continuing is a self-expression class, because of the teacher, Shelley Wolfe.

She was a psychiatrist as well as a teacher, and seemed to have an almost hypnotic sort of hold on the class. She somehow got these depraved people to write some profound stuff that I think even surprised her. I don't know how she did it, but I do know that those were some of the saddest stories I've ever heard. Stories full of drugs, abuse of every kind, poverty, and misspent and wasted youth, often spanning multiple generations. I did notice that she had each of our files with her and somehow she could tell that I was — I wouldn't say "shocked" — but affected by the stories I was hearing. I was just thinking of signing up for more writing classes when… Shit, I just remembered they took my "student" ID for mouthing off at the music guy. Oh well, I wasn't learning anything anyway.

I know, Dear Reader, you've been painfully virtuous, I mean, patient with me, but please consider that I'm not only writing the chronicle of MDC, I am MDC, as much as anyone can be. So, it's all good, or at least it's all valid.

Dave and I stayed great friends after we left Tampa U. I stayed on a year or two longer after he left to go to another school. I never graduated and never went back to school.

Dave's mom never liked me; maybe it was just my intrusive manner and loud motorcycle. My mom, however, loved Dave. I think it might have to do with my mom having six sisters and no brothers, and Dave having six brothers and no sisters.

My mom was an actress and was in a Broadway show for a while. She lived to be 90, and I was glad that she got to know her grandson, Brian, and it was good to spend a little time with my mom during the last five years of her life. She wasn't thrilled when I left NYC to join a punk rock band far away because it was "fraught with peril," but she ultimately supported my decision after she saw the albums and heard about the tours to Europe; it took her a while but she saw the results of our hard work. She probably came to 25 MDC shows in all.

She had a certain amount of theatrical-mindedness having been on stage herself. MDC was playing at the New Music Seminar at NYC's Peppermint Lounge around '86 or '87. We were on a pretty big bill with Biafra, DOA, Samhain, and Celtic Frost. My mom came to the show and afterwards I was looking for her and found her up on the third tier (not to be confused with the tiers at San Quentin), and she introduced me to the person she was talking to, who just happened to be Joey Ramone.

I always kept in touch with her, no matter what. One of my biggest regrets was the pain I caused her when I went to jail. We wrote each other often; truly, prison doesn't do much good for anyone's family. I was 41 when I went to prison; I wasn't a kid, but still, it hurts when people care about you. I miss her to this day.

Once Dave had five of his brothers come to a show at CBGB in New York City. They all came up on stage at the end for the last tunes and sang "Chicken Squawk" and "Folsom Prison Blues" with us. It was a gas for Dave, and made it a memorable show for all. Had Dave's mom been there, she would have loved it. Of course, before there was a band for our mothers to see (or not see), a few more years passed after Tampa.

After I dropped out of school, I was sort of in a limbo of lame-assed jobs. I worked at a place that sold eyeglass lenses, and then at a machine shop. I worked two years in Quebec, Canada. Dave and I always kept in contact though. I moved back to New York City and lived with my mom for a while. Due to my late father's good name, I found myself working for a company that rented the most expensive apartments in Manhattan to the richest people in the world. I was amazed at how many people in their twenties could qualify with incomes in excess of one million dollars!

Although the money was very good, I was overworked, stressed, and miserable. Six and seven figure incomes might have been my coworkers' life goals, but were not necessarily mine.

One night Dave and I went to see two shows of the jazz drummer god Billy Cobham at the Bottom Line in New York. After the early show, Dave snuck into the bathroom and hid in the stall so we'd get the best table in the house for the late show. I went into the bathroom a little while later, not sure that he was there. He was standing on a toilet so that his feet wouldn't show. I walked in, and asked, "Dave, are you here?" Just then, unbeknownst to Dave, an usher walked in right behind me.

"No one here but us chickens... buck, buck," replied Dave and broke out laughing. The bouncer recognized me from the early show, smiled, shook his head, and left.

At the late show, we had the best seats in the house. Our table was front row center, and so close that I could have choked Billy's cymbals. Roberta Flack was at the table right next to ours. At such a close vantage point, the cool stuff that I wouldn't have ordinarily noticed jumped right out at me. Stuff like how a master like Cobham can play so loud with so much power, and so soft and subtle with such control, all at the same time. It was a thrill. Just another exceptionally cool time Dave and I shared.

Then Christmas vacation brought Dave, who was attending the University of Texas in Austin, back to Long Island. Dave brought a tape of the band he was working on with his friend Ron. I knew little of Punk Rock in general and less about what was to become known as

Thrash (that is after I invented it! …did he really just say that?!) I quit my job, much to my mother's chagrin, and flew to Texas with Dave after Xmas break. Being there to make and create music, and only to make, create, and play music, was an exciting new perspective.

While Dave was up in New York, Ron had recruited, at least temporarily, Mikey Donaldson from The Offenders, one of the best god-damn players I've ever played with. And, one four-count later… Well, Dear Reader, you really should've been there.

Meanwhile, let me tell you that we are on lockdown here at San Bruno, San Francisco's county jail. Lockdown is just what it sounds like. A couple of the queens went at it, and we are all paying the price. I won't let it cloud my good news of the hour. That is, I won't be going to San Quentin after all. The bad news is that they are giving me a choice of staying in the county jail for a year, of which I would be required to serve eight months and twenty days, or going to a drug program where I would have to do nine months in-house and nine more out-patient. I would be out of jail though. I wouldn't be surprised if your protagonist ran from said program though. What they call the "play now, pay later" plan. And once out, play it really cool and underground. Below the radar.

Oh! To program or not to program? The program has got to be better than jail. Once in the program, it's "to run or not to run."

Fuck! I love my life, both as a drug dealer, and as a traveling musician and a recording artist. Well, I have the next three weeks to dwell on that decision.

3

Well, Dear Reader, I'm afraid that once again, I have good news and bad news. First, in the time it took to turn this page, seven months have come and gone. I decided to opt for the drug rehabilitation program, instead of serving eight months and twenty days in the county jail. As I said earlier, I wouldn't be surprised if your protagonist ran from said program. Guess what?

I got out of county jail after a few months, was sent to the Walden House drug program, and absconded shortly after arrival. I thought I'd go back to what I was doing but things had changed while I was gone. It was a struggle to drop back in to the life, got caught after seven months, and — long story short — I have a new address. I am looking up five tiers of cells that stretch as far as the eye can see, which is the view from Cell 1 West 28, in the infamous West Block at San Quentin State Prison.

Now, the good news: I will tell you more about Quentin as I learn, but now I have some long days and nights ahead with nothing more pressing or important than talking about MDC back in the earliest days.

Things would be happening fast for us that year for the band that would become Millions of Dead Cops. As soon as I got to Austin in January of 1980, Mikey Offender Donaldson and I joined up with Dave and Ron Posner and played six shows. The very first show was the Texas Farm Workers benefit at Duke's on Congress. If I'm not mistaken, the bill was The Reactors, The Inserts, us (we were The Stains back then), and I got to see for the first time, the legendary Dicks and Big Boys. They were the punk rock mainstays in Austin in those days. I got to meet a whole bunch of great musicians that night. Life was good.

Just a few words about the fellow who was my predecessor on drums. His name was… well, of no real importance. Let's call him "Joe." Now Joe had made it clear to Ron that he didn't know for how long, or really even how much, he actually wanted to play with the band. He had a life with his job at a bicycle shop, and school, and his girlfriend, and a few other priorities that he trotted out for Ron. The last on his list of "Things more important than the band" was his DOG! Fools and excuses are things Ron suffers badly. So, the fellas had no problem relieving Joe of his percussion responsibilities.

Well, the day before the first show, we were finishing rehearsing, putting the finishing touches on our most advanced tunes to date, namely "Born to Die" and "Business on Parade," when Dave get this devilish grin on his face. He grabs the phone and shushes us.

"Hello, Joe? I really hate to ask you this, but, well, our new drummer Al… well, he isn't really as good as we thought, and, well, do you think you might come down to the show at Duke's tomorrow night and bring some sticks and take over if we need you?"

Joe was feeling generous and agreed to help the poor old Stains out in their time of need. Dave thanked him. His face was red trying not to crack up before he hung up.

The next night came around and as were taking the stage, Joe shows up, girlfriend in tow, sticks in hand, sporting a magnanimous smile. Dave gives him a look of acknowledgement and nods a grateful nod in his direction. Thank goodness Joe is here to save us!

We start into the first song of the first set of the first show I would ever play with MDC (not yet our name!) and by the second chorus, Joe has lost his grin and realizes he's been had. He really DID need to bring his own sticks because he wasn't fit to even carry mine. As he slunk away from the front of the stage, his girlfriend turned around and smiled. Apparently, he had spouted off about his upcoming rescue to her and God knows who else. At least his dog was spared the embarrassment. Thank goodness for that! The guy deserved it, what can I say?

We spent a year in Austin before we moved to San Francisco. It was that first tour which made us know the Bay Area was really where we wanted to be. I was living with Franco. He had designs on becoming our new bass player.

We had run up our, that is, *my* phone bill past the point of no return booking our tour, and figured what the hell, it's going to be pulled anyway. So we abused the fuck out of it! I had long, long long-distance conversations with the person who was to be our greatest ally, Jello Biafra.

Biafra was the leader and genius behind, and in front of, my favorite punk band, Dead Kennedys. To this day, I still believe their first album, *Fresh Fruit for Rotting Vegetables*, is the greatest punk rock album of all time. (Author's records and present company excepted, of course.)

When our single, "John Wayne was a Nazi," came out, we had mailed copies of it all over the place. One copy was mailed to *Creep* magazine. Unbeknownst to us, Mickey Creep shared a mailbox with Biafra. Hot damn! Biafra got it, loved it, and contacted us. I couldn't believe it when he phoned to ask us if we wanted to share a bill at the Mabuhay Gardens in San Francisco.

We moved up our tour plans two weeks to accommodate that gig. I still remember the date. It was December 2nd, and we didn't have another show for at least a week. This was certainly a stretch. We talked and talked on the phone for hours, and established a friendship I still cherish today. I will admit to being a bit awed by him and his generosity, and by Ray, Klaus, and Darren. Oh, that Darren H. Peligro... what a drummer! What a band! I know. I'll stop now.

We got to the Mabuhay, also known as The Mab or The Fab Mab, and didn't know where to stay. We had come with our Austin buddies and sister band, The Dicks, in the Dicks' 1967 Ford Econoline van and our guitarist Ron's orange Monte Carlo. We played the Mab, and Dead Kennedys cut us an unheard-of equal share of the pie. The Dicks also got the same. The total sum for the bands was $1200 and change. We each made $400 and something. Needless to say, DKs were the draw, and needless to say how much we needed and appreciated the gesture.

Joe Target liked us and we stayed at the Target Video warehouse a few days. That's where Buxf christened us. You see, we were still The Stains back then on our first tour. That's where we found out about the L.A. Stains. And our next port of call was the Cuckoo's Nest, where Black Flag had booked us with the L.A. Stains! The time had come to find a new name. We were at a loss. "Texas Stains" was one lame suggestion. "Fatal Stains" was suggested by Jello, to which I thought to myself, "Sure, easy for you… your band is the fucking "DEAD KENNEDYS!" That's when I looked across the room at Buxf. That would be Buxf Parrot, the bass player of The Dicks, and a real deal Texas punk rock brother, if there ever was one.

I said, "Fuckin' hell, Buxf, what do you think we should call ourselves?" I probably would have voted for whatever he said next, that's the regard I hold him in. Buxf looked up from his Budweiser and spoke the words that I will never forget: "Call yourself 'Millions of Dead Cops'!" and even as Dave and Ron were thinking of all the implications — scary and otherwise — I KNEW! I FUCKING KNEW!

Buxf sat down and drew on a cocktail napkin the Klan Cop picture that became our logo. Salvation had been found! We knew who we were. For the record and all time, let me state that I was the biggest fan of that name in the band, and would never have broadened our acronym to mean anything else. I still feel that way today.

We were fortunate enough to have some friends in Oakland put us up. (Put up with us, was more like it.) The gig money from the Mab was enough for us, especially with Ron "Ebenezer Scrooge" tight-wadding our bankroll. That was a good thing, too. The Dicks weren't blessed with a crotchety skinflint like Ron, so they drank up their cash in no time. Times got a bit tough. The Dicks decided to leave early and went back to Austin in Ron's car.

The day after The Dicks headed back to Austin, we were hanging out in San Francisco where we had heard of the local legends of the Mission, or the scourge of all punk rock, according to Tim Yohannon of *Maximum RocknRoll* magazine: The Fuck Ups. Either way — legend or scourge — of course, we wanted to meet them. We went to their storefront on Guerrero Street and Seventeenth. We approached with caution, but The Fuck Ups weren't home. Our luck was still holding strong though, as instead we were happy to make the acquaintance of The Fuckettes.

The Fuckettes were not only the back-up singers of the Fuck Ups, they also were the only folks who could keep the Fuck Ups in line… "in line" being a relative term.

We were sorry The Dicks hadn't stayed long enough to meet them. They both had something binding in common, namely, Budweiser. Between those two bands, beer in general didn't stand a snowball's chance in hell. By this time, we were nearing a financial crisis. Salvation was to come once again from a most unexpected source. Upon hearing of our plight, Leslie Fuckette asked, "Why don't you guys get food stamps?"

"Food stamps??? Really?" Why, in Texas, they came to your house, looked in your fridge, and then, maybe, you could get a miserable forty dollars' worth. However, here in San Francisco, one just had to make out a receipt or two to prove or establish residency, and the next day collect $70 in grub stubs. "Why aren't you on the dole? Everybody else is," laughed Leslie.

There were seven of us, and we happily marched out of the welfare office with $490 in wonderful, life-sustaining food stamps. Hooray for the Welfare State! Hooray for food stamps! And double-hooray for The Fuckettes! They saved our asses. Love ya, Leslie, Victoria, and Virginia.

We had arranged some radio interviews in the Bay Area, and one of them was with Tim Yohannon at KPFA in Berkeley. Tim was an older, rather politically correct punk rock radio DJ. His weekly radio show later branched into *Maximum RocknRoll* magazine. We all got along famously, which led to MDC having the privilege of being on the cover of the very first issue of *Maximum RocknRoll*.

Tim was a political revolutionary who had seen and lived the power of music as an instrument of change throughout the '60s and '70s. He was quite different from the Fuck Ups, whom he detested.

Now, we liked the Fuck Ups as people and they liked us. Tim told us of lead singer Bob Noxious's t-shirt that had an unacceptable racial slur on it, and wanted to know what we thought of that. We obviously were opposed to such a garment, and told him so. They never pulled any of that racist crap around us. I suppose it's that "don't discuss politics or religion at the dinner table" type of thing.

I've always felt that whenever someone amends his (or her) behavior when they are around other people because they like or respect those other people, then they are also questioning the belief system that produced the view that they are amending. In other words, I found it to be no surprise that we never heard the Fuck Ups saying demeaning racist bullshit around us. They simply liked us, and sensed that those words weren't going to endear them to us. That isn't to say they were denying anything. Nor am I saying that street punks like the Fuck Ups, or anyone else, consciously — either singularly or as a group — makes or decided to change what they were saying. That's the beauty of it. It's an automatic self-made adjustment in one's attitude due to unacceptability. For example, I think most people use the word "Fuck" a bit less often when their grandma's around. We found out that the t-shirt Tim was referring to had only been worn once and Bob had already ditched it. We never even saw it. Either way, we thought it reprehensible, and let them know so.

Personally, I am over trying to judge everybody, and realize that I am the only one I need to be responsible for, and that I'd do well to be very careful about borrowing any clothes from Bob at any time.

This, however, was our first exposure to the lines drawn indelibly in the sand, between the peace punks (or political punks) and the street punks. On one hand, you had your street punks and the bands they championed like Code of Honor, Verbal Abuse, and of course, the Fuck Ups.

On the other hand, you had the politically correct punks. Some of them have even looked down their noses at us for smoking pot. These political punks were idealistic, peace and love types. They were more likely to be into bands like Crass and Dead Kennedys. They were usually into political literature and looked up to the *Maximum RocknRoll* crowd. We were in the middle.

Many of the peace punks were too sanctimonious. These holier-than-thous mostly lived with Mommy and Daddy, and didn't really deal with the realities of street life any more than they wished to. Again, eighteen and knew it all. They, at least, knew how to go slumming, even if they weren't aware that that's what they were doing. Some of them (a lot) knew their way home to the 'burbs.

The street punks had usually come from more tragic backgrounds, and lived mostly on their own from young ages. Their existence, day to day, didn't afford them the same idealism. They were past the arrogance of thinking they could save the planet.

There were members in my band who had come from both sides of that coin. There was always a healthy debate on the merits and shortcomings of both viewpoints. At some point, though, we decided to agree to disagree. Fortunately, we had much more that we agreed on than not.

Part of being in a band is compromising, probably — certainly — more than you would want. A band is first and primarily a producer of art. There is an infinite amount of combination of notes, keys, textures, and ways to hatch a musical notion. A band is also a business, and a labor (of love, hopefully).

I've often felt jealous of a painter, for example, who has complete control of his medium, his canvas. His only limits are about the edges of the canvas, and the height of his ability.

I sometimes have felt that I was attempting to paint a landscape. I've completed the foreground, grass, trees, bushes all the greens, and yellows, and browns. Alas, when it comes time to paint the sky, some-one else has all the blue paint. Then reality returns to find me having to consult and compromise my art. There is an upside to this required sharing. That is, if I was the lone producer of a piece of art, I wouldn't be able to look to anyone else. Not for support, not for feedback, not for creative input, or just to share an exalted passage, and a shared appreciation for that show, that occasional special show, where everything's happening right.

Sometimes you can throw it all on automatic pilot, and almost watch it materialize as if you're in the audience. Sometimes the drums seem to play themselves. So if I feel that I am putting up with unwanted input (as the blue paint for my landscape) then lack of self-doubt and fear of being too close to be objective, not to mention loneliness at the top, is a welcome exchange.

I do expect that the proverbial grass will always be greener on the other side of fence. C'est la vie, (such is life) or c'est le guerre (such is war), depending on your point of deja vu. (Sometimes I'm so clever I could make myself puke, sorry.)

In the peace punk vs. street punk debate, we could comfortably straddle the fence. After all, if music, and musicians, music fans, and/or the music business as a whole, are the enemy, then MDC doesn't want to fight. It's just another two-plus sided coin.

It's flattering, in a way, to be representative of each group to the other, respectively, while all along maintaining neutrality. While no forum exists between, let's say, the Fuck Ups and Timmy Yo, they both speak to issues worthy of debate. It does put MDC, if not on the spot, then certainly in a devil's advocate position. After all, entertainment is wherever one finds it. MDC wound up asking for it just by the fact that we wouldn't join up with either camp: an unpardonable sin to most people, but by virtue of our being MDC, we were exempt.

"Arbitration, anyone?" No apologies though, to our own selves we could be true. The real enemy came well-armed and dressed in blue.

We finished our tour and headed home to Austin knowing we

would return to San Francisco... to stay.

When we got back home, we decided that the next order of business was to record an album. The next few months were spent polishing old songs, finishing up new ones, and practicing the hell out of all the songs. Ron and Dave had profitable little pot businesses, and I had borrowed some cash from my mom. So, well prepared, we went to a recording studio in Houston called Rampart Studios, and worked with a man named Dan Yainey.

Dan was a bearded, pipe smoking, hippie type in his thirties, and, at first, seemed a bit too reserved. I sensed a bit of that dismissive "it's only punk" attitude. Undaunted, we set up, got levels (a process that painstakingly takes hours), and recorded our first take of the first tune: "American Achievements."

If I was mistaken in my first impression by Dan's subdued manner, I'll never know for sure, because after our first take I could tell that he now was an enthusiastic member of the team. I have since figured out that the tone of any recording session will mostly be determined by the band's very first cut. If the band is tight, and the material good, then it behooves the engineer to work on a professional level. If the band has done its homework, it has the right to expect the studio staff to perform to that standard. This isn't written in stone anywhere (not until now) but it does seem to be something that I have learned to depend on.

It's like a home court advantage, or turning an obligation of running the mechanics of a huge glorified tape recorder into a chance to create, into a labor of love. When this is the case, you'll find the momentum of something that has the studio folks' excitement in anticipation of the hopefully glorious outcome will supersede the immediate need for payment.

Sometimes eight-hour sessions become sixteen hours long with appropriate credit extended, just because the magic is here and now. I think of it as an unwritten law of the studio jungle.

Dan, our engineer, carefully helped us get down all the tracks. I remember the first time I heard the first song in the playback. It was

"Business on Parade." I was thrilled.

Ron, our guitarist, had bought an old Marshall amp that had been masterfully rewired from two channels into one, with an extra master volume set in one of the holes where one of the guitar inputs had been. A short cord connected the second to the third inputs, leaving only the first of the four original inputs vacant. That's where Ron's guitar plugged in. If there ever was an amp that should have gone to eleven, that was it. I recall hearing that rich first chord ringing so brilliantly powerful and resounding with natural vibrato and the fattest distortion I'd ever heard, I'll never forget it. I think that chord dictated itself to the opening song of the album that very second. The rest of the album went along in similar fashion during three recording sessions, and four to seven overdub and mixing sessions.

I, more than once, woke up and ran to my tape deck just to make sure I wasn't dreaming. I was always left smiling, like I'd swallowed some canary. It's still our bestselling record, pushing 100,000 copies, and God (or whoever) only knows how many copies have been recorded on cassette. Punks do that a lot.

So, my friend Redman has been moved to another section and it has me sadly contemplating my surroundings.

San Quentin is no joke. It's immense and strangely lonely, even though West Block alone houses (and I use the term loosely) almost two thousand inmates. I've been here, in lockdown, and time drags on. I've only been let out of my cell to go to chow twice a day. They give you a bag lunch at breakfast, so you don't get out until dinner. The only other times I've been let out was to go to a physical, and a quick shower three times a week.

I'll have to go to "school" someday soon, and then they might move me to another section. "School" is three hours of tests to assist them in figuring out what type of job you are suited for. Imagine, these idiots are going to decide on my employment possibilities. I understand that until you have taken that test you won't be moved out of West Block.

People sometimes stay in West Block for months. God, I hope I'm not stuck in here that long. The boredom is incredible.

While West Block doesn't have anyone with a sentence longer than ten years, many people at Quentin are here doing twenty-five to life… some are never getting out. You sense the gravity of this place everywhere you look.

People are yelling out of their cells on the top of their lungs at all hours of the day and night. I guess it's about 9 p.m. around now, and the 'woods (short for "peckerwoods") are screaming and shouting. Peckerwoods are white boys. Everything here is segregated. The 'woods don't associate with the blacks or the Latinos, and vice versa.

Just before I got here, I heard that four 'woods got "hit." I don't think they meant killed, but whatever they meant, it didn't sound good.

Mail takes three to four weeks to get in here, and it's all read before it gets to you, so I figure I won't have any news from the outside for weeks. The isolation is miserable. I haven't gotten my EPRD (earliest possible release date) yet, and although it's still months away, a date to look forward to would be of some comfort.

I should be getting out into the yard this weekend, but it's only Monday now. Tomorrow will be my eighth day in lockdown in the belly of the beast, West Block, San Quentin State Prison. Talk about being grounded until you do your homework.

Dear Reader, I hope you appreciate the lengths I have gone to in telling you the story of MDC. I've been locked up for three months total to the day now. Two months and three weeks in San Bruno County Jail, and nine days in the pen. I must tell you, Dear Reader, that it could be said that the charm has worn thin. Still I try not to forget whatever so many black men said from ever so many riverbanks up and down the Mississippi, and that is: "You got to suffer if you want to sing the blues." All I'm wondering now is "Are we having fun yet?"

Fourteen songs were etched into a lacquer master disk, and acetates (test copies) were stamped, scrutinized, and approved. Then masters stampers and mothers (a metal copy of the record for use in making new stampers when necessary) were made. Cover art was color-separated and printed along with lyric sheets. J-cards were designed for the cassettes. Finally, all the parts for the records and the cassettes were ready. We were in L.A.; it was 1981.

MDC's first P&D (pressing and distribution) deal was with Tabb Rexx. We worked with him on the release of our first album in the States, and on our second album, *Smoke Signals*, during the recording.

At any rate, after our first album was in the can, we were ready to plan our move west. Ron bought a van that we would use to death over the next year and a half.

So, we loaded up the truck, and we moved to California, just like the Clampetts in the '60s TV show, *The Beverly Hillbillies*. When we arrived in San Francisco, we needed a place to stay. Someone told us about the Vats. The Vats were in a five-story building that used to be a Hamm's beer brewery.

On the building's top/fifth floor were what looked like swimming pools. They measured about twelve feet by fifteen feet, and were eleven feet deep. This is where they mixed up the beer. These, and all the beer vats, were covered with Ebonite, a kind of black hard plastic. These pools led the beer down through a series of pipes to the individual vats below for aging. As one entered the other four floors' hallways, there were five manholes closures on each wall, each one leading into a vat. These holes were used to allow a man in to scrub the inside of the individual vats. At either end of the hallway was a staircase. On the top floor, the entire floor was one gigantic tiled room with a walkway down the center, where the hallways were on the floors below.

MDC lived on the second floor, second vat on left. The vat had walls three feet thick, with no lighting or windows. We ran an extension cord out into the hall to run our lights and amps. Our little hotplate doubled as our only source of heat.

In addition to the pipes from the fifth floor mixing pools, a system of catwalks ran around the back of each vat, and in the back of the whole building. We had to punch a hole through the back of our vat in order to get our musical equipment in, and then build a secure door to protect the equipment.

There were seven of us — four people in the band and a few friends — and our rent for this cold, damp, dark little slice of heaven, in which we could both live and practice, was a whopping $200 a month. Even with such a sweet deal, we still didn't have that kind of money. We were as broke as the day we were born; however, we did have manpower. So most of the time we worked for our rent while living in the blackest caves imaginable. I mean you couldn't see anything.

This building was sturdy. After all, it wasn't built to hold people and furniture; it was meant to hold thousands of gallons of liquid. Twenty thousand gallons per vat, to be exact. Except for the cat walks and the vats themselves, the building was a solid block of cement and steel rebar.

We earned our keep by jackhammering out the manholes, and making them into suitable entrances for people and equipment. First, we would vertically jackhammer the large brass manhole out of the cement. We then would finish and secure the vat by framing the enlarged holes and hanging doors. This was the first step in turning them into rehearsal studios. It was a long and arduous process, but we were glad for work. It was better than getting some straight job, anyway. From a distance, the Vats at Bryant and 15th Streets must have appeared to be a giant five-story block, with holes enough for human habitation of, let's say, the Bohemian style.

MDC eventually moved up to the top floor within a year or so where the mixing swimming pools were, and had it all to ourselves. That was cool.

I had actually moved into a vat on the third floor with my girlfriend, Cecilia. She was a legal secretary with marked punk drummer tendencies. One day, my friend Mia approached me inquiring if I might know a drummer who would like to play for her band, Frightwig. I told her that I knew someone I thought would be perfect, and went home and helped Cecilia sharpen up what I knew was the Frightwig style and feel. She practiced hard, and took the job the way

I knew she would.

I could tell she was more talented than she gave herself credit for, and I was happy to see her blossom to her full potential, not only as a drummer, but as a singer and songwriter as well. I always knew she was a goddess.

Unfortunately, when it comes to women, somehow I never miss my water until the well runs dry; it has been my unfortunate fate to not appreciate what's right in front of my nose. That's something I plan to work on, if I ever get out of here.

Cecilia eventually outgrew me, and went on to light up her own solar system. I heard Frightwig is going to Europe again. It's been quite a while since I've been in contact, so I don't know if Cecilia is still playing with them. I hope so.

Meanwhile, back at Quentin, we've got a serious problem now. I've got some Bugler tobacco, but no papers. I got hipped to the fact that pages of the prison Bible that the Gideons hand out are even the same size as rolling papers. Except for a little ink, they burned as well, too.

So I rolled up a cigarette out of the first page of Matthew. It works! I don't know if I'll ever serve God (Goddess), but now He's serving me quite nicely. Yes, I may burn in Hell someday, but Matthew 4:1 is burning in Quentin (hell on earth) wrapped around some Bugler today.

TO BE OR NOT TO BE, THAT IS THE QUESTION... or was it, "What good does it do to have all the speed in San Francisco if one cannot gettith a hit??!" And (more to the point), "What good will all the speed cash in Frisco do you on the fifth tier in San Quentin?"

4

The Politics of a Front: the Beckoning smile, the Compliance, the Road of Good Intentions that lead to the One Point Seven-five Gram shell game...

One fateful night in 1984, I attended a show at San Francisco's On Broadway nightclub. Some people I knew at the show were selling speed. Now, for clarity's sake, let me define a few terms:

Speed: For the purposes herein, can be defined as methamphetamine hydrochloride, or methamphetamine sulfate, at least, as the main components.

Bunk: That which has been represented as speed, but, in fact, is not.

Speed dealer: The most thankless unappreciated job there is; involves dealing with people who believe that you are making far more money than you are, and resent you for making it. Also, people expect you to be on call 24 hours/7 days a week. The demands on your time and energy aren't worth the rewards. However, a speed dealer is everyone's friend, but only if what he deals in is, in fact, speed (not bunk).

Bunk artist: Rip-off who sells a substitute for speed in order to bilk the unsuspecting speed user.

Front: A credit amount of speed extended to a customer or friend.

However, it should be noted that one might lose said friend or customer simply because the incurred debt precludes him from making his currently desired purchase. Or, at least, making the purchase from you. This, all because (against your better judgment), you did what the customer really, really wanted you to do. This brings me to my last definition...

Joneser: A whiner who can't accept "No" for an answer.

Anyway, now that we have a few definitions, I can proceed with the story.

I'm at the On Broadway, and there are few speed dealers at the show. The ones that were there sold out very quickly, and that, of course, opens the door for the scum that preys on the hopes and needs of the drug-using public. Well, my dear friend Heidi got some of the aforementioned bunk, and had to leave the show sick. The lowlife who perpetrated this fraud was the notorious Nick the Dick.

After that, I wound up going to my connection a total of five times during the show (which was Social Distortion, by the way). I missed Social D but at least no more of my friends got sick from Nick.

On my last visit, I asked my connect, "If I had spent these $120 all at once, how much speed would I have gotten?" She told me that I could have gotten seven or eight quarters for $110, and really you can eight quarters or .22s, and nobody notices 3/100's of a gram difference. You'll make $200 on a $110 investment. So went the introduction to the elusive game of time, patience, and discipline.

The clock starts when you pick up a "sixteenth" (one sixteenth of an ounce). The object is to make back your copping money before you do the dope. There are eight quarter-grams in that sixteenth. One only has to sell four and a dime to get a whole new turn! Easy... right? Like a shell game or the game of Three-Card Monty that asks the participant to "Find the peanut under the shell..." or "Find the queen after I mix the three cards..." or "Find $110 (at least) at the end of your potential $200 venture," and, like many before me, I was on my way to a new second career.

Gee, that seems like so long ago. From purchases of quarter-grams to half-pounds of outrageous methamphetamine sulfate or hydrochloride. Glass and Sparkle. Wonderful stuff!

It's about 2 a.m. here at Quentin, and there's some hick-ass jerk singing sad country songs down the tier. It's got the blacks howling and hootin'. God, I'm glad he's not my celly.

Somebody should shoot him and put him out of his misery... our misery. Man, that off-key, twangy-voiced son of a bitch is fucking awful. I wish he'd (as we say in the pen) rest his neck. Or cut his throat. All just another day in paradise.

After we'd established our home in the Vats, we installed a phone. Besides our usual names, we told the phonebook people that we had a roommate named David Charles Millions. So, in the new phone book, to find Millions of Dead Cops one would find us listed as Millions D.C. We were so clever back then.

After acclimating ourselves to being full time "Vat Rats," we immediately started back in to practicing and getting ready for our next tour. Although we didn't know it then, this would be the longest MDC tour ever. It included four months in the States and Canada, and as we later found out, would wind up taking us to Europe for the first time. The total duration of this tour was six and a half months. We played an average of five days a week. It was too damn long!

So, bright eyed and bushy tailed, we set sail and headed south on the first leg of our odyssey. Our first port of call was the ever-punk, rock mecca, L.A. Our first show was at the famous Whisky a Go Go. Back then, the Whisky had a marquee made of lights that formed words. The words came around the corner. I'll admit feeling a little pride as I watched a big "MDC" come across the marquee.

We were there playing two shows with DOA. Legal Weapon was the opener. When DOA played their first set, the stage-diving was full on. I attempted to catch someone who had done a forward flip from the sound tower. I got him, no problem. I was a bit drunk and having a good time, when I saw another diver headed my way. This time, however, it was me who got caught. Right in the side of the head with the steel toe of a Doc Marten boot. It knocked me for a loop.

So, Dear Reader, if you ever find yourself hurtling through the air because of diving off a stage and look down to see me, check yourself, 'cause as sure as the L.A. sky is blue, I'll be clearing out of your way like the Red Sea did for the Jews.

Well, I've been in San Quentin in lockdown for the last eleven days. Tomorrow will be the first time I get to go to the yard. It's just a small yard with eighteen hundred motherfuckers in it, but I'm sorely looking forward to some fresh air and sun. One learns to appreciate small favors around here. Anyway, that's tomorrow, and tomorrows stack themselves like footsteps on a road to a destination not in sight, not even in sight from the horizon or the next.

Time isn't something that passes here. Here, time is done, or is something you do. Thus, the expression "doing time." I'll now shift from the hard time I'm doing now, to the good times that feel a thousand paces and a dozen crossroads behind me from here.

Before we left L.A., we needed albums. We didn't have time to wait for the pressing plant to press them up with their backlogged schedule. There was only one option. Sunday morning, seven o'clock, hungover from a two-show Saturday night, seven squinting, disheveled, weary northern Californian punk rock musicians and crew crawled out from under our rock de jour, and braved the intense L.A. sun. We met with the pressing plant's owner, and then we lined up with the help of the foreman. We had to man the machines that took a hot glob of black plastic, pressed them into hot disks, and stamped the grooves onto them. From there they moved down the line, where we affixed labels on each side and let them cool.

The plastic wasn't the only thing melting. It was so fucking hot, I couldn't believe it. Meanwhile, the noise and the heat were just what the doctor didn't order for my poor throbbing head.

The next stop for our records was to be put into a paper sleeves, and stacked next to the cover fabricating machines. These machines attached the slicks — cover pictures printed on shiny paper — to the cardboard. Another machine fabricated the cardboard with the slick attached into a cover or jacket by folding and gluing.

The next step is to stuff, by hand, the sleeved disks into the fabricated jackets, and send them through the shrink-wrapper where cellophane is snugly wrapped around the finished product.

We then packed them in boxes of twenty-five and boxes of fifty. We finally loaded them up in the van and prepared for a long trip to El Paso, Texas.

Before leaving for Texas, we had to stop at Ralph's supermarket. We had brought our appetites, but with only the amount of money we needed for gas, we had to be inventive.

I was always the shadiest looking of us, from my skinhead and tattoos, to the dog-chain squeezed around my neck with a vise grips. A big earring and punk rock sneer added to my delightful persona. The MDC M.O. was that I, Al, would enter the market first. I would walk from one corner to the opposite at a speed sure to alert security to my unsavory presence. From there, I generally headed to the meat department.

Nobody was into eating meat, so it was a smart place for the decoy to cause diversions.

About then, Dave and Tammy (Dave's girlfriend, and probably the best manager we ever had) would enter and head away from where I was. They, of course, were dressed for shoplifting success, and would start their first sweep.

Meanwhile, I would start my little act. This consisted of moving slowly along the meat case, grabbing an expensive piece of steak or something, anything will do if it's expensive. Then I would open my leather coat while looking up at the two-way mirrors. I would pause, count to ten, then put the steak back, and move to another area of the store where my comrades were not, and repeat my act there.

Sometime during this period, Franco, our bass player, would enter wearing his perfectly suited long green "magic" coat. With this coat, he could steal juice by the gallon, and never take his hands out of his pockets.

Tammy and Dave, by this time, would have stuffed half the store into their clothes. Then, calmly as a clam, we would walk to separate checkout lines where Franco would buy some granola, I would buy a pack of smokes, Dave and Tammy would buy two loaves of bread, and we'd go out bulging. We'd then rendezvous back at the van, where guitarist Ron would roll his eyes, in a gesture of superiority, as if he couldn't believe it really happened.

A quick high-five between conspirators, and we'd drive off enjoying our cheese, pickles, lettuce, juice, hot sauce, etc., etc., all bought for the cost of a pack of smokes and a couple of loaves of bread. We brought this skill back to San Francisco with us, where Dave holds the record for stealing thirteen vegetarian sushi rolls from Rainbow Grocery.

Dave was to work there many years later. I came to write the first song written by me without any collaboration, "Kleptomaniac," about those adventures:

> It started out of necessity,
> 'cause we were broke and hungry
> But it's not that way today.
> We just don't want to fuckin' pay
> 'Cause I'm a kleptomaniac
> we're all kleptomaniacs
> never gonna give it back,
> Hey, asshole, what you lookin' at?

A true booster's anthem. Hell, it may be after the fact but, at this point, let me be indulgent and dedicate my "Kleptomaniac" to a master shoplifter and good friend, Alan. (Again, I hesitate to mention any last names to protect the guilty). Alan was the one who convinced me to put my stuff in storage before the flood of fair-weather fuckers that fleeced me upon my bust showed up. I saved countless items as a result. Thanks again, bro.

After stocking up on provisions and gas, we drove through the night to El Paso, and arrived at the club. I don't remember the name of the club, but the gig I remember well. Nobody had heard of us there. We wound up feeling like Spinal Tap.

The crowd was out of the '60s, or something. Cardigan sweaters, and I'm sure if we looked, we'd find argyle socks to match. Richie Cunningham comes to mind. They found us equally weird. In addition, the military was well represented. There were about fifty of them. We started to play, and they just stared at us.

Now this was 1981 or '82, and they had never heard anything like us before. Suddenly, they decided to do "The Worm"! I think they were just trying to make fun of us, but after Dave joined in, we all had a great time, and by the end of the set, people were shaking our hands, and telling us how much they liked it.

They moved into the modern age of music that night, and broadened their Elvis Costello, Pretender-ish point of view. We were glad to win these folks over, for no other reason, we knew, like Sinatra, that if we could "make it there, we'd make it anywhere." Hey, we may not be Sinatra, but two of us were from New York, New York. How about dem Yankees?!

Our next stop was Austin. Returning as prodigal sons, rather than everyday home-towners, we were treated with new respect and appreciation. It was very gratifying to be over the competitive band nonsense. We stayed with Dicks' bassist Buxf and Cindy Melbe, a great friend and long-time supporter. The only thing one must remember around Cindy is to finish your beer. Those foolish enough to open a fresh Bud with their half-empty can right there would certainly get an earful. Wasting beer, in their house, was an unpardonable sin. All part of their charm. We love those guys and always will.

I stayed over at Randy Biscuit's house. He was the lead singer of the Big Boys. They helped set up the show for us and shared the bill.

Their ever-enlarging die-hard college and punk crowd was, as always, a perfect complement to ours, and another successful night resulted.

Back at Quentin, my celly Chris and I are twisting up a wick. A wick is a folded-in-half piece of toilet paper, drawn and twisted like cotton yarn in order to keep a smoldering light going. In West Block, San Quentin, lights for cigarettes can get scarce sometimes, and our neighbor with the lighter was "rolled up" or moved. So it is incumbent upon us to keep an eternal cigarette flame burning.

To make a good wick takes two people or else it unravels. As I tried to twist one alone, my celly demanded, "Gimme that pathetic thing," and proceeded to try and fix it. He then informed me that I was twisting it in the wrong direction. I said, "Oh, great. It's a right-handed world, and even fire's a righty."

"You left-handed?" Chris asked.

"Yes," I replied, "but I play drums right-handed though."

"How come?" asked Chris.

Somehow, I knew that the story of my learning drums was germane to this book. It really hadn't occurred to me before. Well, I told Chris, and now I'm telling you.

Many years ago — oh hell, it was 1967, and I was thirteen — I took lessons from a fabulous drummer named Louis Nazaro, in New York City on 72nd Street and Broadway. I asked him about switching around the drums and playing lefty. All one would have to do is switch the toms on the kick drum, and move the bass drum and hi-hat to the opposite of what they were.

Louis hipped me to why that would not be the smartest thing to do. He also made me realize how being lefty was the best thing to happen to me.

"First of all," he said, "if you want to be a session drummer who does multiple gigs in a day, you'll be playing a lot of different kits. Some are pre-miked from previous sessions. All these kits — no matter what trap kit extras they might have — they will all be set up in the standard righty way. There are no lefty pianos, no lefty saxophones, no lefty trumpets, violins clarinets, cellos, flutes etc. That's the bad news. Now, the good news is that you can make this disadvantage into an advantage."

I was working out with dumbbells for some extra arm strength, and Louis suggested I do three times as many repetitions with my right arm as my left. Same for stick control exercises. This program held me in good stead, as the more I played the more I worked my right arm.

The bonus was that no matter how fast and powerful my right arm became, my natural left was already there. This gave me greater speed, more power to my rolls, and gave me an approach to accents that is the most notable characteristic of my style.

I consider myself to be a "lucky lefty" due to learning to take this to my advantage.

I needed the extra power, anyway, being rather slight… all right, I'm skinny, and always have been. Some people have implied that speed caused me to be thin. The truth is that I've never weighed more than one hundred and fifty pounds in my life. Not until now. Here, in prison, where food is everything, I stuff myself from boredom, as well as hunger. I now weigh one hundred and seventy-five pounds, and I look like a roly-poly orange bowling pin.

Another strange thing about reception at Quentin is the fact that here in West Block, nobody's been endorsed to their permanent facility yet, so nobody has a mirror. I saw my own face only twice in the whole 67 days I was in reception.

Boy, by the time I got to see myself in a full-length mirror, I was at my final prison destination of Coalinga. Man, did I get fat, and that little mustache I was sporting in county jail covered my whole upper lip and most of my lower. I looked like a little Italian organ grinder, all gut and mustache.

5

Well, back to the story of me as the mean, lean, percussion machine. We had worked our way up to Chicago after playing Austin, Houston, and Dallas. I can't recall which cities we hit, and which we missed, on this particular tour. Let's just say that we have hit every one of those Midwest towns at one time or another, and most of them three or four times.

So there we were, on the outskirts of Chicago for a couple of shows. One club was called Exits, the other was a theater called The Metro. I wish Dave were available to check my memory on those club names. Dave's long-term memory is extraordinary. Please note: I mentioned long-term memory, and that while I did say I wished Dave were available, I didn't say I wished he was here.

Before we got into the traffic jams around Chi-town, we stopped at a Mexican restaurant called Campeche. Now, Ron was always headstrong. The unshakable confidence he had was, at times, an asset, and, at other times, an onus to us and himself in general.

Today, it was a source of amusement. We entered the restaurant and sat down, with chips and hot sauce already there on the table. Now, Franco, being of Spanish descent, tried a chip dipped in sauce.

"Shit! This stuff is brutal," he said, meaning it was brutally hot. Well, Ron was from Venezuela, and he knew everything anyway. He proceeded to scoop a huge dose of sauce on his chip. The one from the bowl, not the one on his shoulder.

"Not too hot for me!" he quipped. Suddenly, his eyes got big and teared up, then he slapped his index finger against the others, as was his habit, making a snapping noise and exclaimed, "Shit! Shit!" as he bailed for the bathroom, full speed, for some water. I laughed till I cried. Here, once again, was Ron freely expressing his superior right to be dead wrong.

In other cases, there was infighting. Sometimes it was a bit too outward and personal to be contained "in the family" though. The fight that comes to mind was in a laundromat in a black section of Chicago. We were there to do our wash. I'm afraid that our "dirty laundry" consisted of more than clothing that day. The funny thing was that it was an artistic difference of opinion. It wound up, though, like wild dogs fighting over a bone.

The argument was about two songs: "Kleptomaniac," the song about our shoplifting sprees, and a song written about our sad experience dealing with the Bad Brains and their very ugly brand of racism, sexism, and homophobia. It was entitled "Pay to Cum Along," but if I had my way it would have been called "Pay to cum in H.R.'s mouth," for I could tell not only did he suck, he swallowed.

The argument started when Ron claimed that my tune "Kleptomaniac" sounded too much like the Dead Kennedys. I was the biggest DKs fan in the group. Now, I was saying that it was sounding that way because that's the way Ron was playing it.

In a band of three instruments, the instrument that is not the bass or drums is about seventy-five percent of the musical spectrum. If that happens to be guitar, particularly guitar, It's more like ninety percent.

So, as long as we were at our worst, taking each other's feelings to task and reducing logic to a shouting match, I figured I may as well counter his offense with a plagiaristic accusation of my own.

Ron and I avoided any attempts at communication with sensitivity by politely using phrases like "influenced by" or "has a feel like," which could be misconstrued as a helpful or constructive suggestion. No, we (Ron) preferred to say things like "ripped off" or "stolen," which implied premeditation, as well as suggesting that there was a victim. Why not milk a half-valid criticism for its whole bloody worth?

So I made a counterclaim about the song that eventually became "Pay to Come Along," claiming that it was blatantly and maliciously stolen from the Bad Brains.

Well, this fight was major, even by our standards, with name-calling, threats, and clothes throwing. We quickly cleared the laundromat of the other patrons, who bailed when the bailing was good.

It was just another rude childish display of tempers that lacked any semblance of constructive criticism. As I recall, nobody won that argument, but by the time we got those two songs to the recording studio, neither song sounded like the bands they had supposedly been ripped from. They now can be found alive and well, one on the B-side of the "Chicken Squawk" single, and the other on the *Rat Music for Rat People* compilation.

I came to realize that, although painful and brutal at the time, sometimes communication takes on a regrettable form. Sadly, I don't think Ron knew how to express himself any other way. I am, though, glad for the outcome, however it came to be.

Back in my humble little 140-year-old cell, Holy Shit! They scared the fuck out of me. I had taken an HIV test, and this morning I got this "Priority Medical" slip. Of course, I'm thinking the worst. Especially since I was told that if you're HIV test comes back positive, they call you in right away, within forty-eight hours from when you were tested. I had gone to my physical exam the day before yesterday. I went to the lab feeling sad, lonely, just this side of suicidal. Man, in prison, and now AIDS.

At least I was rubbing elbows with the big shots, for I turned around upon hearing someone yell, "Escort!" This, I found out, meant that you were supposed to stand against the wall until the prisoner requiring the escort was passed. I looked up to see this little man in a yellow jumpsuit. He glared me and hissed like a snake. It was then that I recognized him. My god, it's Richard Ramirez, the motherfucking Night Stalker. Hissing at me like a devil. I sneered back at him. What, was I going to get scared and upset about some noisy little mass murderer? Not me. Especially with a four-man escort, not to mention the fact that his hands were chained to his waist chain. He was so bound up, it reminded of *Silence of the Lambs.*

The creepy feeling Ramirez gave me made me forget my own nightmare for a second. Not much longer than that, though. I was sick to my stomach, and practically crying, thinking — I should say, dwelling — on the mess I had allowed my life to become. I thought about my kids mostly, as I waited in line for about a year, and then, I couldn't believe it. They just wanted more urine.

Urine! I know HIV tests are blood tests. Thank God (Goddess), and Hail Satan. Urine! I never considered the musical quality of that word before. I still don't know why they needed more piss, but it was surely not to test for AIDS.

They may take a few months from me at this end, but at least I know I'm clear of a death sentence at the other end. Boy, those CDC Corrections Officers and the medical staff at Quentin can't help themselves. They just have to have their little joke. Like Don Adams in *Get Smart* might say: "I fell for the old forty-eight hours medical slip trick."

Like the song "Maria" in the musical *West Side Story*… "Urine, I just got a test for Urine. And suddenly that name will never be the same to me. URINE!!!!!!!!!!!!!!!!!!" (Very cute, Al, where do you come up with this stuff?) I don't know, Reader, but aren't you glad I do?!

6

I have in front of me a huge list of memories compiled during the last few weeks. Each is a place and a story. MDC has played so many shows in so many places that, by this point, fifteen years later, I have only my memory to rely on.

I also feel that it is only fair to acknowledge that my recollections may differ from other members of the band, both in content and point of view. However, I do attest to everything I write as being the truth the way I remember it, and not varnished. I do not deny or defend my right to editorialize at will.

Mostly, I mention this now because, for the life of me, the chronology of many events is lost to me. We have toured so extensively, and over such a long period of time — from 1980 to 1994 — that a lot of the order of events is unclear in my memory, especially earlier on. However, I don't believe that whether any particular event mentioned herein took place on our third or fourth trip to Europe, for example, is of the utmost importance.

What is important is that they did happen, and I hope these events are of interest and amusement to the reader. (... Always thinking of you, Dear Reader.)

While we' re on the subject of stuffy disclaimers, disclaiming stuff, this review from Canada basically tells us to get stuffed. You know what a sick puppy I am. It's one of my favorites.

The show was in Ottawa, and the publication was the main daily newspaper of that town. *The Ottawa Whatever* or something. It was the sort of paper that has the same posed close-up of the writer next to every by-line they write.

This reviewer, Ellen Somebody, had long blonde hair and a pouty little smile that just made you want smack that cutesy little sorority self-assured grin off her snooty, snotty little face. You know the type.

The correction officers, sweet and helpful as they are, are not likely to let me go to the library to look it up verbatim, so as close as I remember it, it went:

Last night I saw the band Millions of Dead Cops at the Wave Club. They played too fast and sounded too loud and noisy. Not music at all. The lead singer stomped around the stage like Charles Manson on bad acid. I couldn't stand it. I had to leave. These guys should be shipped back to California in lead cages.

Now, me, I'm the sort that would be dying to check out these "lead cage Mansons," so, to me, it's a good review that would entice me to go to see MDC, especially when you consider that Miss Thing, who wrote those glowing expletives, would definitely not be in attendance.

Something I've learned about promotion and press is bad is much better than none. Not maybe for one's ego, but for business. Any mention puts you in the public eye, and, for better or worse, that's where you need to be. Certainly, it's not like, "If you can't say something nice, then don't say anything." That's good manners, not good promotion. I believe that we still use that review in our press kits.

This reminds me of a little saying I used to have: "You don't have to tell me if someone's an asshole. I'll figure that one out myself? But PLEASE feel free to tell me if someone's a thief. I'd rather not have to make that discovery on my own."

Furthermore, since my recent discourses with the law, I've enlarged that saying to include: "PLEASE, PLEASE! Tell me if someone is a snitch. Man o' man, I fuckin' don't want to learn that the hard way!" Yeah, I'm rambling again.

Meanwhile, back on the road, we heard that the Kennedys were going on tour in Europe, and were planning to bring a support band (that's what they call the opening bands over there) with them. Gosh! Europe. We immediately phoned Biafra, and, as only we could, asked — ASKED, did I say "asked"? — I meant to say *begged* to get on that tour.

We found that he was considering bringing Flipper or DOA. We kind of realized that we were a little out-classed by those older, more seasoned bands who probably deserved a shot at Europe more than we did. At the end of the phone call with Biafra, we at least got our name into the hat.

Older, seasoned, more deserving or not, we were still sharp, well-practiced, and most of all, hungry. We called Biafra every other day from wherever we were playing. I'll bet our nickname around them was "Millions of Annoying Pests," but, of course, Biafra was always in-terested in our progress around North America. If nothing else, it was a good barometer as to the state of punk rock in general. At any rate, we made sure that Biafra knew how badly MDC, or MAP (Millions of Annoying Pests), or whomever, wanted to go. In retrospect, we were like little kids trying to talk Dad into taking us to Disneyland.

"Oh, we'll pay our own airfare, Biafra. Oh, we'll sleep on floors, Biafra. Oh, you can put our album out on your label in Europe. Just give us the shows. Just give us a hundred or two a show, and we'll handle the rest. Oh, please can we go? Can we, please? Can we, huh? We won't be any trouble."

It was like the cartoon where the chihuahua is jumping all over and around the bulldog with the derby hat, saying, "Gee, Spike, whad-da we gonna do today, Spike? Can I hang around with you, Spike? Huh, can I, Spike? Can I?"

As ridiculous as it seems looking back at it now, it worked! One day, when we called in our normal every-other-day report from, ironi-cally, London, Ontario… well, Spike, I mean, Biafra, told us that soon we'd be visiting London, England. We were really happy. Six weeks later, the Kennedys and the Annoying Pests would be on our way abroad.

Unfortunately, there were unseen crocodiles in the waters immediately in front of us. Your heroes, Dear Reader, were not out of the dark forest quite yet. Au contraire, not the four stooges of punk rock! Hell, we could fuck up a wet dream, and Murphy had plans for these lucky Europe-bound Dead Cops.

Our schedule took us back up to Toronto for some shows, and we were holed up there for a couple of days. We had run out of pot that first day, and with Europe to pay for, money was extremely tight.

Well, Ron and Franco had managed to hoard a joint out of our band stash.

Dave asked, "You guys got a joint?"

"No," came the reply. Somehow, Dave and I had a feeling that we weren't getting the straight dope. (No pun intended… well, maybe just a little.) Ron and Franco then took off to do some mailing or something.

The next thing we know a mohawked guy named Mike is telling us a tale of how Ron and Franco double-parked in front of the main post office on Queen Street, a major thoroughfare, and had been busted for the pot they had told us they didn't have.

When we called down to the police station, we found out our selfish little pot-hoarders were charged with possession of marijuana, and upon searching our vehicle they also charged them with possessing a weapon dangerous to the public good, or something like that. This fearsome weapon turned out to be a dog chain left over from when we used to have my Doberman, Glove, on tour with us.

Furthermore, having found literature from the John Brown Anti-Klan Committee, not to mention our albums and buttons, all embossed with the name "Millions of Dead Cops" and our half cop/half Klansman logo, we were now considered a seditious organization.

Canada doesn't have the same Bill of Rights free speech protections as the States, and even if they did, we weren't Canadian citizens anyway.

The John Brown Anti-Klan Committee's platform contains planks about the possible violent overthrow of the government of the United States, among other things, and we were closely aligned with them way back from the Texas days. The Anti-Klan part of their trip was what we were in sympathy with, especially in Texas. No matter what they think in Canada, in Texas, where the hooded Klan members are often seen riding around in police cars, John Brown can use all the support it can get. This, however, was the backside of that two-edged sword, and would cut deep into MDC both now and for years to come.

Dave went to see about getting our van back, and returned white as a sheet, having been given the same sort of treatment that the Smithtown and La Grange cops had given me only months earlier. They really didn't appreciate the humor in our name.

Well, maybe they did. After all, they refused to return our "Dead Cops" buttons. Perhaps they just wanted them for themselves, and their friends and families. We were lucky to get our van back at all. We missed two Toronto shows, and were in a kind of a limbo.

I walked all the way to the C.N. Tower by myself that night. It was about three to four miles away. I left at three o'clock in the morning, because I couldn't sleep. I just walked, and considered the gravity of our plight. I approached the tower and found I had it to myself. Sometimes one needs to be alone with their thoughts. Privacy is a rare thing when you're in a band on the road. Then I realized that I too was in danger of being arrested because of my affiliation with this seditious MDC organization. Did I mention that our work visas expired on the stroke of midnight? After that, we were illegal aliens.

The next morning, we regrouped, and moved to houses on the outskirts of town. During this time, we employed an attorney. Andy King was the lawyer's name who secured Ron and Franco's release. He also helped us get our visas updated through the US embassy.

Apparently, we should have gone to the US border, crossed it, and returned for Ron and Franco. Well, that sounds fine, except we couldn't be sure that we would be allowed to return after all the trouble we had supposedly caused.

Boy, talk about your expensive herb! That pot those fools wouldn't share with their own band members cost us seven thousand dollars in lost guarantees, merchandising, and of course lawyers' fees.

Of course, we never got our t-shirts, albums, or buttons back. I didn't really expect that we would. Like I said before, we were probably lucky to get out of Canada with our instruments and our van.

While we were sitting on our hands waiting for news of our naughty string players, we made a discovery. Boozecans! In Canada, all liquor and beer has to be purchased through a government outlet beer store. These close at five or six p.m. The bars all must close at midnight. So when the twelve o'clock police nazification occurs each night, the party goes underground.

A "boozecan" is a speakeasy. It's just like Prohibition in the '20s, without "The Untouchables" or the bootleggers. My favorite boozecan (we visited three or four) was called The Liberty. I like the sound of that. It was a huge warehouse, where the beer and drinks were served from a huge elevator. If, or when, the cops showed, it was "illegal beverages going up" to the second floor where they could be quickly unloaded and stored safely, legally before the Keystone Untouchables could bust it. Ingenious.

Looking back, it seems that with a crowd of such size, at such late hours, somebody also must be paying out for the privacy it seemed to enjoy. What reason did I have for thinking that the police in Toronto were any different than police everywhere else? All pigs, all corrupt, all on the take in one way or another, and none worthy of anyone's trust. Fuck police everywhere!

We regrouped with renewed travel (not work) visas, and were exhausted as we crossed the border at Detroit-Windsor… or I should say, Windsor-Detroit? and we were glad to be home.

Yum! Just got back from another scrumptious gourmet meal at Chez Quentin. They had a dinner they jokingly call "Beef Wellington." To me, it tastes more like "Beef Waterloo." If Napoleon had served this to his troops, he certainly wouldn't have had to wait until Waterloo for Wellington to beat him.

Now, if Wellington got a taste of San Quentin's "Beef Wellington," he'd turn over in his grave, or if he wasn't dead already, this stuff would kill him. Either way, he'd at least want to change his name.

Every night, after dinner, from some cell upstairs, a black guy always yells the same thing: "Well, gentlemen, it's another day without pay. You don't lose your bitch, you just lose your turn." At this point, Dear Reader, I can't tell you exactly why, but I find this pronouncement mildly reassuring. I guess I'm getting institutionalized. Maybe not. Oddly enough, no sooner have I put this down on paper, then he got moved to another section. Although we will keep the tradition alive, I don't think anyone will say it quite the way he did.

True, I find the term "bitch" offensive, but his manner of saying it had a feeling of affection. His voice has a tone of a belief that someone will be waiting when he gets out. Someone soft and feminine, yet hard and strong. Someone who will help make sense of all this. Someone to celebrate his freedom with.

To me, this person's name is Mayginn (her own spelling). She is half my age, but is ageless. I've never felt that way about anyone before. Well, at least, as long as I remember. She's a freckled-faced redhead, adorably skinny and small breasted (which is my preference). I didn't know that until I met her, either.

Mayginn is clearly not as enthralled with me as I am with her. She used to be a couple of years back, but I was too smart. I treated her badly, and have been working my way back into her affections for about two years now. I ran around on her, and we constantly fought. I took her on tour with us in the States, and even then, I didn't treat her like the goddess I've since discovered she is.

We lived together for about six months, and got used to each other. Oh, when I think of the times that we scrounged around for a quarter-gram here and there.

Then, when we were going to Europe, I refused to take her. I consider that to be one of the biggest mistakes of my life. I was no sooner in the car headed for the airport when I realized how much I missed her. How I loved and still love her. But I was too smart for my own good. I wasn't going to take that brat to Europe and give up those European women.

Well, I had the most celibate tour of my life. I'd be someplace wonderful, like the mud baths in Copenhagen, Denmark, girls all around, and I would smile and miss my Mayginn. I miss her right now. I know she hasn't been involved with anyone, and I guess it's a comfort to think, even if she was, that I wouldn't lose my Mayginn, even if I do lose my turn.

Mayginn does have a new friend though: Mr. Heroin. Although I know anybody with heroin as a friend will always have their own agenda, I feel that I fucked up so much in this relationship that I've decided I have to love her the way she is. Not that she has any plans to give it up anyway, so she winds being a bit expensive, too.

I sometimes feel that I built up my little (not so little) meth empire just to impress and share with her, much as F. Scott Fitzgerald's *Great Gatsby* did for Daisy. I only hope, in time, she'll forgive me, and we don't end up as tragically as Fitzgerald's characters did.

Now, I know sometimes she's working me. I don't mind, as long as she knows that I know I'm being worked. When she starts to think that she's getting over on me, and that I'm not keenly aware of it when it's happening, then I'll feel like a sugar daddy. I think she knows that would make me feel weary and old, and I'll surely stop helping her. The fact that she hasn't found someone yet is all the encouragement I need not to give up.

There, dear Mayginn, you got me to spill my guts and show the world just how much I care, and in what high a regard I hold you. All out there on Front Street, for everyone to see and know.

Thanks for putting up with me, Dear Reader, and now as we say here in Quentin, "I'll rest my neck now."

7

Well, we made it back down to Austin, where we could lick our financial wounds, and kick back a few weeks before we had to be heading back to San Francisco.

We rebooked the next month of shows as best we could on such short notice. Fewer shows, smaller guarantees… not the optimum situation. We did the best we could, and filled the rest of the money obligations from record moneys, and a loan here and there.

We got back home to San Francisco, played a few local shows, and without time to unpack, had to leave for New York's Kennedy airport, bound for London's Heathrow airport.

We had set up gigs in New York. The City (New York City, of course) also afforded us lots of different places to stay. Dave and I, being from the area, could get out of the loop to go visit hometown friends and family.

We had shows at CBGB, and Gildersleeves, and an all-night bar called the A-7 2+2 Annex. Its name came 'cause the original bar was on Seventh Street and Avenue A in downtown Manhattan. The same folks had a dungeon on Second Avenue and Second Street. The A-7 2+2 Annex was much larger.

One night, someone broke into our van while Ron and Franco were asleep. The thief grabbed our boom box and our tapes, and was high-stepping, heading down Fourth Street and around the corner of Avenue C in downtown Manhattan. He was probably "getting his hit" while Ron and Frank were finally getting dressed to… to do what? I know, it's not really funny, but the thought of Ron and Frank standing in the street in their underwear and socks, cursing the junkie who was undoubtedly laughing as he cooked down his shot, brings a chuckle to mind. You boys ain't in fucking Kansas anymore, Toto!

This little annoyance could only stifle our excitement for a short time. We had a world to conquer. MDC was well practiced and sharp as a tack on your teacher's chair. We were extended to the max, and quite in debt. We were wide-eyed, naive, and a bit scared as to the degree of acceptance we would enjoy. These four California fish were certainly going to be out of their element.

I'd only been to Europe once before, but only in Spain for a week, and I was a child back then, with my mommy and daddy. So, really, I'd never been anywhere in Europe. I don't think any of us had. Yet there we were, on a 747 headed east-northeast, unstoppably bound for fame and fortune (or folly and ruination). We surely felt a bit strange not having our own van, without our own equipment, and being totally dependent on the DKs.

We had given Biafra the right to press the first *Millions of Dead Cops* album to make the whole two-band tour thing work out to be a justifiable expense. We hoped that this would pan out for us as well. MDC wasn't used to putting that much of our fate in anyone else's hands. Well, we had decided to, and even begged to do it this way, and hell or high water, it was going to be our biggest adventure yet.

How unbelievably strange it seemed back then; I want to say "foreign." Now, having gone over there eight times total, it seems so comfortable, even mundane. The truth is that the first and last tours to Europe, for all the difficulties that might have occurred, were my very favorites.

The first for the sheer wonder of all the sights and cultures. And the last because, to some extent, on the last tour, you see, we conquered Eastern Europe, including being the first western punk rock band to ever play in Russia.

The other thing that made the last tour my all-time favorite was my being able to bring my young son, Brian.

None of these things would have been possible without that first tour, which only happened thanks to Jello Biafra.

Christ, more accolades, how will I survive? Oh, Poor Reader, I suspect that somehow you will. I see how much you are appreciating my little preface. So, without further ado, let's move on!

8

We landed safely at Heathrow Airport, London, England where we met our European record guy in the person of Bill Gillium. It was a sunny day, and Bill was in good spirits. He gave us a run-down of our itinerary. We had a John Peel session on the radio, as well as the eight or so British gigs. He drove by some of the sights including the BBC (British Broadcasting Company). Yes, reader, I thought you probably knew what BBC stood for.

We wearily arrived at a hotel called the Columbia, where reservations had been arranged. All in all, everything appeared to be in order, and we were happy and impressed.

We found out that our first show was at the intimate London Musician's Collective. It was supposed to be MDC and Dead Kennedys, but at the last moment Biafra lost his passport. The Kennedys, all of whom were in England on time except for Biafra, had to cancel. Fortunately, the hall was small enough that MDC was enough of a name, or at least, enough of a novelty, to fill it.

The Kennedys took the opportunity at sound check to practice, with or without Biafra. I guess they were entitled, since it was all their backline. (The amplifiers and drums on stage are referred to as backline. Maybe you didn't know that, huh, Dear Reader?) The Kennedys hadn't just come off months of touring, as we had, and had to "find the hard groove." Happily, that groove is never too elusive to people who have played together as much as Ray, Klaus, and Darren.

In the absence of a lead singer, who could fill in? Who knew the words? You guessed it! And, as the man said, "You do the driving, I'll bring the beer!" That's right. Bet your missing passport that Al knows the words, and how to count the measure, not to mention giving the rest its full value. They were impressed by my knowledge of their lyrics, and a surprised DKs had a good time when they were expecting drudgery.

I have always been moved by the power of music and lyrics, but when some German people, who spoke only broken English, sang us a few lyrics we had written some seven thousand miles away in Austin, well, the feeling of satisfaction was indescribable.

At the show, we couldn't have been more pleased if the Queen herself (God bless her and the Fascist Regime she rode in on) had stopped by, than to have Steve Ignorant and Phil Free of Crass in attendance. Hey, whaddaya know? They liked us and even extended the very rare invitation out to Issington to the Crass farm. We had always been, at least, curious and sometimes fascinated by these famous provocative Anarchists, who have reached across time and space with sanity and conscience. I guess they felt that we were still worthy of saving, or maybe worthy of being shown that there really is an acceptable alternative to the American Rock'n'Roll Machine. We accepted their invite, after all, the Kennedys hadn't been invited. We arrived in Issington at the farm two days hence.

We had anticipated the normal band to band pleasantries and stories and banter, but found ourselves — I wouldn't say "on trial" or in a fish bowl — but I did feel as if we were being sized up as to motive, method, and content. I think it sounds creepier than it was. In a way, it was kind of flattering. I felt that they were just cautious about the company they kept.

It seemed to me that their questions could be construed as fodder for over-intellectualizing (where the hell did that come from?) but it was more figuring out if we were your average American, me generation, short-sighted big shots. In short, they wanted to know if we were about anything at all.

Some members of Crass were having a lot of trouble with our

name. Crass, as we knew, are pacifists. No justification was going to change their minds about the fact that the name "Millions of Dead Cops," to them, represented violence. That's not to say that they were naive, but they live in a country where the cops look more like firemen. This was the most interesting thing we debated.

Unfortunately, as a result, Dave decides that he can't hang with who we were. Our name had to change was the opinion that was gaining support either by collusion or by abstention. I watched in horror as we rethought our position and watered down our convictions, and found myself unprepared for a debate that I had no warning was to take place. I believe that if Crass had any idea how their opinion was going to sway us, they would have not been so vocal. But how could they know? Especially since I didn't know myself.

It took years to get back to the original meaning of MDC. In the meantime, nobody would mourn for that name more than me.

Now, Penny Rimbaud, drummer and — as it appeared to me — Big Daddy Crass, related a story about a band he was recording down at Southern Studios in London. Penny was talking to his second engineer. He was just commenting on how he thought this song was a classic. The musicians involved overheard, and held that to be the Gospel, and made much ado about some comment made in haste.

The exact nature of the story I don't recall. The point, to me, was obvious: in this case, it would relate to trusting one's own judgment, and appreciate the wide and varying circumstances by which we arrive at the conclusions we do… or… the places we've reached… or…

Just because they're Crass doesn't mean, in or of itself, that they are right. And Penny Rimbaud of Crass himself is telling us this.

Another subject at which we found the answer to be original, if not unexpected, was touring. Crass said they were only out to make an impression on, or have an influence in changes and appeals for sanity in their part of the world, and weren't interested in touring America. They didn't believe an American tour could even be worked out on their terms.

That money hungry, star-maker machinery behind the clubs,

bars, and theaters, and the music industry backed by big business, to them and us too, is the height of hypocrisy to a political band.

We left late that evening with a heightened awareness of what a European independent's definition of success was. After a long heart-felt debate, we concluded that if we wanted to address issues and be taken seriously, we couldn't always be voicing ourselves through "Millions of Dead Cops." We had been feeling the two-edged sword of carrying the flag of Millions of Dead Cops, and a little change without compromise sounded inviting. No more border panics, no more having to be extra nervous around police (I've always feared the police, natural born enemies). No more pseudonyms like Matt Dixon and the Confederates, or Mint Double Chocolate, or My Dog Charley.

It was that day in England that I thought of Multi-Death Corporation, singular not Corporations, that was one of Franco's bad suggestions that he pushed through strong-arm style. (By strong arm style I don't mean physically, I mean by manipulation.)

Our next project was to be about atrocities presently occurring in South America and El Salvador. We were using photographs of people who had murdered, and had their faces burned beyond recognition by acid. These pictures had been smuggled out of El Salvador and given to CISPES (Citizens In Support of Peace in El Salvador.) Had the smuggler been caught, it would have been more likely than not that he himself would have ended the same as those he photographed. This subject matter and literature was far more suited to a record by the next manifestation of MDC.

Once again, music and politics were joining people together in a humanistic endeavor for a cause of supreme importance. CISPES helped us design the jacket, which unfolded into a poster for the "Multi-Death Corporation" EP.

The front cover was a drawing, and a concept depiction of the Skull Tank, logo of the Multi-Death Corporation. The Skull Tank was exactly that: a part-skull, part-tank crunching through a field of children, grimacing in pain. That was the outside cover. The smuggled photos and information were the inside. I feel that it was shocking yet dignified, and was a project I was proud to be part of. Crass liked it too, and put it out in Europe on their own label. It was the first American record to appear on Crass Records, a fact of which I'm equally proud.

Meanwhile, back at the London offices of Alternative Tentacles (Biafra's label), all was not well. Biafra, having replaced his passport, arrived to find that not only wasn't his record out, but the ten-page book that he and Winston Smith had laboriously designed to be included, had been clipped a half-inch all the way around. "Holy Spinal Tap, Batman!"

This would further delay the release. They would be touring an album that was not yet available, *Plastic Surgery Disasters*.

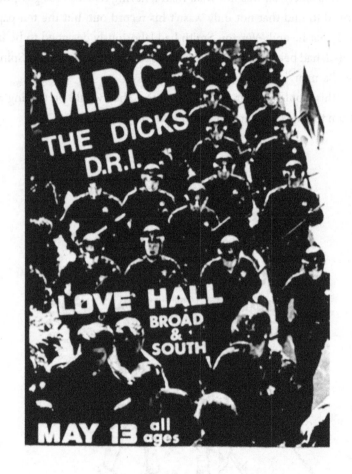

Jello Biafra, now he's a complicated cat. He has been put upon and challenged so much in his career, that in public he calls on — or crawls into, depending on your point of view — "the Biafra persona."

Biafra is a quick thinking, arrogant quipster. The persona is immune to personal attack, and stands above all on an egomaniacal platform of political commentary, and rock star unapproachability. He's often clumsy, in that he frequently steps on toes without realizing it.

Don't misunderstand me, though, I love Biafra. Especially since I'm aware of the gentle side. For the purposes of this book, when I refer to the flesh and blood behind the star, the "man behind the curtain" behind the Wonderful Wizard of Oz, I'll use his initials, EB.

I'm not sure if EB will care for my forthcoming disclosure. I'm sure the Biafra persona will not. Either way, I want it known that I mean no malice toward EB. I've seen people shaft him and malign him for who he is, and I know that the platform from which he talks down to the world is also the life raft that keeps his head above the jaded sea of those who would be glad to see him fall. I was glad to have seen EB, and not only the Biafra, and I empathized with much of his pain.

I do know what it's like to be plagued by a jealous, condescending public. I do know what it is to have your heart broken by dissension within your own band to the point of treachery. I truly did suffer when I saw the mess they had made of his booklet in Plastic Surgery Disasters.

I watched his marriage decline and disintegrate, and the frustration of his inability to do anything to stop it.

Yes, much of the general criticism of Biafra is valid. Much of it is just part and parcel of having the political conscience, and being the undisputed Crown Prince of punk rock, second to only King Johnny Rotten Lyden.

While some of the complaints are deserved, one should appreciate the Julius Caesar-like environment, which led to that insensitive callousness.

As moths are drawn to fire, people will always gravitate to Biafra for what first attracted them. That is his genius. That is, he is truly brilliant and that he really cares. While Biafra shrugs off any criticism and appears aloof (that's his job or reason for being), EB internalizes every negative word. I watched him suffer indignity at the hands of those who should have helped him and supported him. I recall, late in the tour, mentioning to him that I had finally got to hear their new album. He shocked me when he looked away from the rest of my band, looked me straight in the eye, and asked in a meek, high-pitched voice that was only characteristic of the vulnerable EB, "Passable?"

I told him honestly and reverently that what I liked on the album, I really liked.

Nowadays, we rarely see each other. When we do, I'm pleased to say that the same mutual respect and admiration for one another, and for each other's work, has endured. I also find that he has reconciled the man and the image. It makes perfect sense to me, and was the natural progression of things.

Now, some thirteen years after that trip to Europe, the man isn't so sensitive or thin-skinned, so the persona need not carry the heavy shield of protection. Furthermore, the pain and insecurity have given way, as time has healed some wounds and put many more in perspective. Since we first met on the telephone fifteen years ago, he has been through divorce, financial ruin, and many levels of betrayal from within and without. He has made records that pushed the First Amendment to its breaking point, to strengthen it, and, when being part of a band wasn't working for him, he did the most thought-provoking brilliant spoken word I've ever heard.

With well over one hundred records (viruses) on Alternative Tentacles, and a firm grip on the independent side of the music business, that arrogance has mellowed into self-assurance, and he has nothing to prove, not even to himself.

So allow me to take this opportunity to thank you, Biafra. You gave us Europe, and at least a dozen other shows, put out our record in Europe, and treated me and mine as friends. I'm proud to say that at no time did I join in the Biafra bashing.

I learned early on that I didn't have to hear any "news" about anyone in punk through the jaded, malicious rumor mill. After all,I was Al MDC, the most famous nobody in the welfare line. Your original soup kitchen celebrity.

For example, this one time, the "news" was out. Henry Rollins was kicked out of Black Flag. I believed it. Why not? Why would anyone lie about something like that?

Well, Dear Reader, I'll tell you why: take a group of street punks sitting in, let's say, the Compound, on 16th Street and Albion in SF, in 1984. Young people without a lot to do. So, they're talking, just talking. One has a tale about Joe Local and his whatever, while another has some dirt on, let's say, Ian MacKaye. He begins with the catchall phrase, "Well, I heard…," and suddenly he's the center of attention, so it grows, and before it's through, it goes: "Man, that Ian Mackaye! I heard that he's selling heroin at the Congressional mall, and he gets it through the Tim Yohannon *Maximum RocknRoll* connection. They get only the best; the purest brought over in record boxes for Alternative Tentacles by Jello himself. And, as you heard last week, Biafra won't settle for second shelf. No, only the best grown and processed at the Crass farm will do."

You get the idea. There's a great deal of jealousy, and there's some feeling that the Punks somehow own a piece of a band that they used to like before they "sold out."

So this make-believe stock these people have in these bands gives them some right to have opinions of importance, and make judgments. Most of these verdicts will find the poor band guilty as charged for the crime of selling out. I say to any and every band that, sooner or later, whether or not you do something to deserve it, one or more of these parasites will go out of their way, in the name of self-righteousness, to painfully ask you why… or tell you that he used to like you, until you… sold out!

Well, as it happened, we had some business with Chuck Dukowski of Black Flag, and their label SST Records, in Redondo Beach, California. So I called down there. Guess who answered the phone?

"Well," I said, surprised. "Surprised to hear your voice, Henry. I heard that you were kicked out …eerrr… had left Black Flag."

"Oh, really?" Henry replied, then turned away and covered the mouthpiece. I heard him laughingly ask, "Hey, you guys, are you guys planning to throw me out?"

We all laughed, but I learned to check the source if you want the real story. Henry said at least he wasn't dead like last week's rumor. I was very embarrassed.

There is another reason one can't believe everything one hears or reads. Some people derive satisfaction, even pleasure, from the misfortunes of others. Indulge in another's pain. Biafra has had more of that than anyone I know, far more than he deserved.

10

While on tour in Britain, we played a show in Sheffield, an industrial city in the Midlands. It's a grey, depressing sort of town, kind of like Detroit.

Sometime before the show this thirteen-year-old kid asked us if we needed a place to stay overnight. We weren't sure what to make of this very personable young man. He told us that his mom wouldn't mind, but he would call her up just to make sure we would be welcome. I figured a long shot, at best. Well, he comes back, and it's all good. We stayed over at their modest little apartment.

Franco and I talked with his mom all night. She was hardly older than us, anyway. She told that his father had left them recently, and that her son had just changed schools, and that he was having trouble making friends, and was sort of lost and lonely. One has to wonder how he got to the show alone in the first place.

We decided that we were going to take him to school the next day. His mom smiled approvingly. The next morning, bright and early, we drove to the main entrance of the boy's school. (I apologize for forgetting your name, kid, but should you read this, give my best to your lovely mom.)

Once there, we armed him with an album and cassette, and an MDC t-shirt which he proudly put right on. We pulled right up to the front, all got out of the van to say goodbye, giving him high-fives, and loudly making a fuss in front of half his school.

The kids stood wide-eyed in amazement. Then, off he went as a sea of young teenagers swallowed him up, bombarding him with questions about who we were. We could tell that this little display wasn't going hurt his making friends, and, after all, any friend of MDC is a friend of MDC! As we drove off, he waved, and we waved back. I remember thinking this was like a movie or something. It made me feel good for the rest of the day.

On another night, we stayed at Rob from the Amebix's squat. He was quite punk, with a chicken bone braided into his mohawk (or Mohican, as they call it over there). I remember discussing subjects like the dole, and squats in Europe as opposed to America. I told him how I was kicked off welfare for not sweeping the streets. He and his drummer Virus (also drummer of Disorder) couldn't believe it.

"Didn't you all go down and cause a row? That's out of order. If they ever didn't give us our dole checks, we'd all be down to burn the fuckers out proper."

"What about the police?" I asked.

"They know better; they want us to get our dole money, too. It saves all the trouble of us robbing and stealing for our pints every night" they laughed.

The same was true of the squats. England has a housing shortage, and rather than kick poor people out into the cold, damp British night from old abandoned houses and buildings, the police would prefer to stay uninvolved, if possible.

Evictions did occur at the building owner's request, but police would often have to stave off rocks and bottles, and they would avoid it, wherever possible. We found this attitude all over Europe.

We would discover that, while many things are similar throughout Europe, especially in comparison to America, many things were staunchly different, and the different countries relished these differences. For example, when we left England, we took all our bags and guitars and stuff on a train. The train went onto a ferry, and then continued once we reached the mainland of Europe. All of a sudden, we are in a World War II confrontation, complete with well-armed Nazis (sprecken no English) from the customs department of Germany.

They came into our compartment like we were Jews in Warsaw. These boys were, unlike the British police, well-armed with everything but a swastika. They looked just like Nazi stormtroopers. They were rude, loud, and only spoke to one another in an angry-sounding German.

They tore through our stuff, and held on to our passports for what seemed like hours. Finally, they begrudgingly gave the passports back to us, and we figured we were home free.

About a half-hour passes, then they're back! They told us to pick up our bags and follow them. (Their English had returned, at least enough to order us around.) We couldn't believe it. They had us carry everything we had to the very last car, and proceeded to search it all again. They had us empty our pockets, and checked our passports again. Then they opened Ron's guitar case, and found a small vented disk.

"Ah-ha!" they exclaimed. They now had the dope. We tried to explain that it was not cocaine, as they had thought. The word "cocaine" was now in their ever-expanding English vocabulary. We told them that what they had there was desiccant, used to keep the guitar dry in humid places. Fuck, it said DESICCANT right on the thing. Finally, they had to admit, if only to themselves that they didn't have anything but what amounted to musical mothball. As unapologetically as possible, they left us alone in the last car of the train. I half-thought that they were going to disconnect the car and push these punk rock Americans over a cliff to help save the world for their fuhrer. *Sig heil!*

II

However, the fun was just beginning. When we arrived in Hamburg, our first German gig, the taxi pulled into what could only have been police headquarters. There were forty (we counted) green and white VW vans with German eagles, and the word POLICIA written in gold letters on the doors. We had arrived at the hall!

(For clarification purposes, on our first tour to Europe, we played on the DKs' backline, and only had our own personal baggage and guitars.)

There were over two hundred policemen assigned to the show to control this crowd of maybe fifteen hundred. Gee, we felt like we were in LA again. Hey, maybe they were just trying to make us feel at home! At any rate, we felt "secure," ha ha.

Another stark difference was the PA and the PA crew. It didn't seem to matter if the speaker cabinet contained two six-inch by two-inch tweeter horns or two eighteen-inch low end woofers, the cabinets were the same size.

These cabinets were meticulously stacked in two columns on each side of the stage. They stood eight cabs high and two abreast, looking like two monoliths from *2001: A Space Odyssey.*

After the show, the PA stacked up in the truck with equal precision. The truck fit the PA exactly. We half-expected the road crew to goose-step when they packed it.

When we showed up at our next gig, in Recklinghousen, we were informed by the promoter that we were twenty minutes late for sound check, but it was all right. I thought to myself, whatta guy... "It's all right!"

The funny thing is, he wasn't being unfriendly; he was just being German. I love Germany, but some of the Germans have raised anal retentiveness to an art form. I wish to mention that this German-means-anal thing doesn't universally apply to all Germans. Just the ones who find it objectionable (only kidding, ha!). Still, the trains DO run on time.

Back in Recklinghausen. The hall here was quite unusual. There was a huge pit between the stage and the audience. It was like an orchestra pit in which the floor had been removed.

The place was called The Rotation, and as near as I could figure out, the stage must have revolved, and down in the pit must have been the machinery.

Now, Dave is a powerful figure on stage. In fact, I remember some people being violent at The Farm in San Francisco, at a show with the Dicks opening up for us.

Some "pit thugs" were "blindsiding and cheap-shotting people," as Dave would say, in the pit in front of the stage. The Dicks had stopped playing because of it.

Dave, with a smile, calmly takes the mike from Gary (the Dicks' singer), saying, "Excuse me, Gary," and turns to the offenders in the crowd, asking in a normal speaking voice, "Who the fuck are you?"

Then, having gotten their attention, he — I don't want to say "shouted" or "yelled" — more voluminously repeated himself two or three times.

"You paid, so you think this is your show? You think you have the right to fuck people around, you little shits?!"

While the three or four skinheads were obviously shits, they were by no means "little." I'm like "Fuck, it's on now!"

Dave then violently shuddered, as if he were looking for something to punch, then turned red and got all puffed-up, looking like he was going to spontaneously combust or something.

He, then, again — "shouts" is not the word I seek — proclaims

loudly, "This is MY FUCKING SHOW... MY FUCKING SHOW!"
It put me in mind of a charging bull enraged.

"And here's your eight bucks!" continued Dave, whipping a bill
from his jeans, and snarling, tossed it at the creep who had come to
the front of the stage. "Now, why don't your assholes GO THE FUCK
HOME?!?"

The crowd went wild with approval, and I could see that everything was going to be all right. I can never think of a time when I was
prouder to be in MDC.

This, however, was not to work out so nicely with this pit between
us and the audience. Dave's rage — or outrage — was wasted in Recklinghausen. This orchestra or machinery pit might have protected the
Kennedys from their audience, but it had kept Dave from protecting
ours from this asshole. In fact, this guy looked Dave right in the eye,
and proceeded to punch a girl in the face, giving Dave a "whaddaya
gonna do?" glare. All we could do was stop frequently, and play an
abridged set that night. We never got over caring about the people
who came out to our shows (even if they really came to see the DKs).

Meanwhile, at Quentin... It's Saturday and they have a new game
for us West Block guests. You're locked up like an animal all week long,
and, of course, everyone's dying to go out in the yard. This privilege is
allowed on Saturdays and Sundays in West Block.

The new game????? No Yard!!!! Ha Ha!! Well, I follow certain
rules of survival that my dear Clarissa gave me. One is "Don't let them
beat you by depriving you of telephones, canteen, or yard."

Anyway, I'll have been three weeks here in West Block on Tues-
day. They should be moving me soon. The place they move you to is
the same. I could be sent to any one of three sections of South Block.
They are called Alpine, Badger, or Donner: A, B, or D.

The C section is Carson. Carson is for those serving ten years on
up, so I'm pleased as punch not to be going there. I pace the floor, and
wait for the next one hundred and fifty days to pass as time drags on.

One of the little ironies I'm experiencing here is that there is no music in here, except for some very marginal amateurs. However, there is no lack of immature, violent, filthy, sexist, rap crap, and, in fact, it pounds at all hours, and makes me not only miss my freedom, but hate this place more and more.

West Block, San Quentin, Dear Reader, is a hot, loud, ugly little slice of hell, and is to be avoided at all costs. I make my bed neatly almost every day. I try to keep this nasty cell as clean as possible. I feel it helps me. It's sort of a cross between Betty Crocker and Hannibal "the Cannibal" Lecter, from *Silence of the Lambs*. I try to keep myself elevated above this generally lowest common denominator of humanity. I know behind the faces in here are to be found some of the saddest sets of circumstances in the world. Degenerates who find it totally acceptable to refer to women as "bitches and ho's" constantly.

They even don't have respect for their own children. I heard a man bragging, "I know that baby's mine, the little nigger look just like me."

My celly Chris asked, "Did you hear that? That guy just called his own son a nigger," and laughed. I laughed, too. What else can you do? The one that I couldn't believe is when I heard a guy say, "Hey, man, all the brothers gettin' locked up, I have a seventeen-month-old girl, and I'm worried that she ain't going to have no one to fuck when she grows up."

I couldn't even laugh at that. It didn't make me feel angry. Angry at who? The depraved, deprived source of that statement about his children? No, not angry or even sad or disgusted. It just made me feel empty, and oh so tired of prison.

Now, even most of my dreams are filled with police, jails, and prisons. Sometimes it seems like I wake up from a dream to find myself still in a nightmare. I guess I have relatively little to complain about with the average sentence being over three to five years, up to nineteen, to life sentences.

There was a man who gave us our Intelligence Quota tests. He's been here for thirty years. My God, Thirty Years. I'll shut up and count my blessings now.

It's about 10 p.m. here, and a shrill-voiced loudmouth is talking about players and bitches and ho's (oh my!), and about how good she sucked dick, and on and on.

It's now the next morning, and I'm here to tell you that bastard kept me up almost the whole night. Now he's lost his voice. It's now a gurgling little whisper that sounds like a girl. There is some justice at Quentin, and I'm glad, for I sorely am going to need the sleep tonight.

The next morning I got to go see my counselor. He's a stone-faced, clean-shaven reject from the police force. The bottom line is that I have thirteen points. This puts me at a level one.

Level One is minimum security. That means a ranch or a CCF (Community Correction Facility), or someplace where I can do my time without too much drama. I also got my EPRD (Earliest Possible Released Date), although it's only my third-time. I'll get my half-time when I reach my mainline institution.

The third-time date is October 11th. I'm sure I will get a date in September sometime. October 11th, the day before Columbus Day, which is also my mom's birthday. Five hundred and four years after Columbus discovered America, about as much as a New Yorker discovered Miami when he flies down for a vacation.

If we're talking history, San Quentin opened one hundred and one years before I was born. Back in 1853, when a prisoner was released, he got a horse on which to ride out of the gate, with a rifle and a twenty-dollar gold piece.

Nowadays, one gets two hundred dollars of gate money and it's a rifle-less, unarmed, bus ride back to San Francisco. That may be far less romantic, but I'm sure that freedom is just as sweet.

It's only April now. October is a hundred years away, but I tell myself, I knew the job was dangerous when I took it! It sounds like James Fucking Bond, huh? Like when Goldfinger said to Bond, "No, Mr. Bond, I don't expect you to talk. I expect you to die!"

Well, six months is a long time, but I don't think I'll die.

West Block to West Berlin... Smooth transition. Yes, Reader, I think I'm getting the hang of this writing stuff.

Back in '82, there were, of course, still two Germanys. In order to get to Berlin, one had to travel through East Germany taking a road known as a "corridor." There were three main corridors going from West Germany to West Berlin. These corridors were fenced in and heavily patrolled, to make sure nobody escaped to the West.

There was no doubt that you were leaving the West and entering a Communist country. The people in the Intrashops, government-owned gas stations and store, all wore uniforms and equally blank expressions on their faces.

They weren't going to the party in decadent West Berlin with all its exotic craziness. They were going home to their state-owned little house or apartment, decorated with the few commodities the state would allow them to have. Some of these Intrashop workers seemed angry. Some seemed just resigned, but few seemed hopeful of any change occurring in their lifetimes. No one had any notion that the Berlin Wall wouldn't last the decade. All seemed apprehensive about anyone from America.

We arrived in Berlin without incident. Our friend had arranged for us to stay at the Rausch House. The Rausch House was a squat that used to be a convent, now inhabited by people who needed housing. They had organized, and had fought an eviction for years. They had painted, restored, and basically renovated the building. When push came to shove, they barricaded themselves inside, and when the police came, it was suddenly raining bricks and rocks on the invading police. Instead of the good old LA "call out the helicopters, tear gas, and SWAT teams," the government decided to give up, and even gave the people the right to be there. They turned on the power and water, and set up an agreement, by which maintenance and upkeep of the building were left to the inhabitants.

The German government now gave the building a designation as a registered squat, and the tenants, with whom the agreement was signed, were named as the caretakers of the now landmark building.

The Rausch House was the first such Registered Squat in Berlin. To us, as Americans, coming from a country where they'll do anything from call out the National Guard, to drill holes in the roof in winter, to rid empty buildings of squatters, this seemed the most civilized thing we'd ever heard. It demonstrated a different side of Germany than the Railroad Nazis.

We went up to the third floor, and over a bowl of hash, I asked, "So, where is the Berlin Wall?"

They laughed, and directed me across the hall to the bathroom, and told me to look out the window. I did just that, and discovered that the Rausch House bordered directly on the wall itself.

Now, the Berlin Wall was something. It was actually two walls, with about thirty yards of no man's land in between. In the middle were these huge metal crosses on their edges at close intervals. These were to prevent tanks and other heavy weaponry from crossing. Directly across from me, with my third-floor view, was a machine gun tower. Another tower loomed about one hundred yards away. I couldn't tell you, or even imagine, how many people lost their lives fleeing to freedom in the West through that forbidden zone. I can't even imagine the desperation that would drive someone into such a deadly place. The zone was also mined, as well as guarded.

Funny, the walls surrounding the main yard here at Quentin look so like the Berlin Wall as seen from between the two walls. Double walls with a naked no man's land in between, and manned gun towers just waiting for a chance for some target practice. In East Germany, I'm sure, like West Block (or should I say "Vesten Blocken"), no warning shots are fired in that "unit" either.

Maybe, I can almost imagine their desperation. When the Wall went up, people were separated from their loved ones, probably forever, and well, I know being separated from one's family is an unbearable heartache, worthy of taking supreme risks to quell.

In here, at least, there is a light at the end of the tunnel. Still and all, escaping over the Quentin wall or the Berlin Wall would seem to me to be equally perilous.

While I was surprised by the lack of late night things to do in Europe in general, this was not the case in Berlin. After our gig at a hall called the So 32, we found several all-night places to dance to all different kinds of music. It was the first time I ever heard Grand Master Flash's "Don't push me cause I'm close to the edge!" I remember thinking it was a rebirth of musical black radicalism. It was refreshingly reminiscent of the Last Poets or Gil Scott Heron.

This was our (my) first exposure to rap music. Berlin was also my first exposure to Nina Hagen's music, which took me a bit more time to appreciate.

I've long since stopped claiming to have a valid musical opinion. Sometimes music I felt was not good wound up being the most successful. So, who was I to be critical, although many times people wanted my opinions. I resolved to say that I was not a critic. People make their entire gig out of criticizing others' music. I've come to think that in that dissection and close critical evaluation, the soul and mystery are obscured along with the enjoyment of the whole. I preferred to avoid that burden. After all, I'm just a drummer. Dave, however, was (and is) quite the opposite. He was glad to voice his opinions, mostly compliments, on different bands or music. Biafra also tossed out accolades at the drop of a hat.

One time, I heard Dave telling a singer that his band reminded him of Flipper and Black Flag. He had meant it as a compliment, and actually was quite accurate in his assessment, as I remember that I thought they did sound Flipper-esque. Ted Falcony, a good friend and guitarist extraordinaire of Flipper, will love that word, "Flipper-esque."

While Ted might love it, and it was meant as a compliment by Dave, the singer's face dropped. He apparently not only didn't agree with Dave's opinion, but not liking Flipper, he was devastated, and here was the singer and stage leader of MDC, and all it represented, making this unwelcome comparison.

At some point in time, I even stopped watching the opening bands, because the volume and energy of the performance often would drain me of energy.

For a while, I would lie when asked, "Did you like my band?" I'd say, "Yeah man, it was cool," or something to that effect. After a while, I decided I hated lying, although it did matter how disappointed it might have made someone in an opening band, someone who probably liked or loved MDC, and wanted me to see his or her performance. I'd be painfully honest, explaining how it was a working night for me, and my main responsibility was to give the best performance for the people who paid to see us. I would then tell them that I would love to see them play on a day when I didn't have to play afterwards. If that didn't work, I would then explain that I was kind of tired, it being such a long tour (which was always true) and playing five to seven nights a week. Most people can relate to that, and if I was to watch the opening bands, then I would be too tired to give my best.

I think most people appreciate not being bullshitted. I do know some people misinterpret my absence as some kind of rock star snobbishness, but I forgive them. After all, they're only mere mortals quivering in the shadow of my glorious light. (Only kidding! Boy, this guy's a laugh a minute.)

It may appear from this story that Dave was insensitive, but it's really quite the opposite. He never picked apart anyone's performance, and often hung through opening bands just to promote good will, even when the band was lackluster.

That was also part of Dave's tireless persona. He is a big, kind of swaggering teddy bear. Dave has always possessed a magnetism that was there way before MDC. Somehow, this could be a two-edged sword at times also.

Dave was the guy who would be chosen by the wise guy, or the drunk, or even the mugger who happened to get on a bus filled with people. Without saying a word, the character in question would single out Dave to approach. Dave had more drunken strangers, who knew nothing about Dave and never heard of MDC, telling him their sad life stories. For no apparent reason, Dave was the one the angry guy, or whatever creep was in the vicinity, would hassle.

In Europe, they do know who Dave is, and they do love to drink.

Consequently, Dave spent many an evening in Europe with piss-drunk punk rockers, when I think he would have preferred to be elsewhere.

Dave always had the same charm with women. For an average-looking guy, Dave's had some beautiful girlfriends. Fortunately, Dave, for the most part, is an honorable nice guy who never considered women, or their affections or feelings, as something to be trifled with. I like to think I learned a lot from Dave Dictor in that regard. In the same way, I appreciate our audience.

My father used to say to me, "Alan, if you deal with things like housing, food, or clothing, you have to have a different sensibility than if you are in a business that doesn't deal with necessities."

My dad co-oped buildings for a living in Queens and Brooklyn. Way back in the '40s and early '50s, the American dream of owning one's own home was dying in New York City. A handful of landlords owned most of the apartment buildings and people, more or less, had to pay rent all their lives. My father and a few partners, in an idealistic way, decided to buy a building, own it for ten years or until the principle and mortgage were paid off, then eventually sell it to the tenants as a cooperative.

He would, however, retain the management contract for ninety-nine years. My dad and his partners then would use the funds, and do the same thing again, with another building or buildings. This was far less lucrative than just holding on to the building and collecting rent, but it would allow the tenants to own equity in their building, instead of flushing all their hard-earned money down the greedy landlord drain.

I know what you're thinking… What the fuck is Al going on about now?… Well, you don't have to use that language in your thoughts, and I'm about to tell you. Forgive me if you've figured it out already.

Now, I was in the business of making, selling, and promoting records and tapes. These were certainly not necessities. You could not live in a record. You cannot eat or wear one. You wouldn't suffer from not owning an MDC cassette or t-shirt. People support our trip and music by buying our stuff from appreciation and love. I never, nor will I ever, forget or under-appreciate that fact. I don't even mind when people re-record our stuff on cassettes… not that it would matter if I did. However, when I go to someone's house and see our music in their rack of tapes they have recorded themselves, I do feel especially offended when the tape owner accuses us of "selling out."

MDC has never made more than a marginal living from our music, at the best of times. We have tried our best to stay out of the "Rock and Roll machine." So, when some know-nothing thinks we've gotten too big, whatever that means, and says we have sold out, I'm likely to reply, "You sold us out to Maxell and Sony and TDK, or whatever two dollar-a-dozen cassette company. I don't care that the sound quality is inferior, or any of that arty stuff. It is more the blood, sweat, and tears that have gone into MDC."

The other side of the love/hate relationship between MDC and its audience is the people who think our music is an excuse to stomp around the pit "cheap-shotting" people with a license and right they've bought at the door for the cost of admission.

There are actually people who think that they take MDC more seriously than I do. Some have the nerve to think that they have the right to. Amazing, to my way of thinking. I'm reminded of a time we were playing at the Nottingham Co-op in Madison, Wisconsin.

I'm sitting outside, next to a couple of young guys, and I hear one of them ask the other, "Hey, you going in?"

The other guy says, "No, man, I hate MDC!"

I asked,"What do you hate about MDC? I mean, that's a pretty strong word. What did MDC ever do to you?"

He looked at me puzzled. I laughed, saying, "That's okay. I'm only kidding," and extended my hand, saying "I'm Al Schvitz of MDC."

His friend said, "Oh, man, you're the drummer." I confessed to being the drummer, and told them I'd see them inside. His friend looked at me, embarrassed at his little faux pas.

I said, "Come on, you guys, I'll get you in." I was later to see them on the side of the stage, rockin' and a rollin', and all smiles. I guess he didn't hate us as much as he thought, or even enough to cheat himself out of having a good time.

I'm hoping, Dear Reader, that my ramblings and rantings are of interest. I know what my father did for a living might be off the track, and my view of relevance might raise objections in a court of law, but I think it's all germane if you really want to know the what and why of how MDC thinks and feels. So, Objection Overruled.

If you are noticing that my apologies to you are becoming more sarcastic, so am I. It's not that I'm being any less sincere or honest, it's more that I'm beginning to feel a little more comfortable with my writing. Now, my little notes to you, Dear Reader, are more to clarify than to bias my shortcomings.

I'm certainly not as comfortable behind a pen and paper as I am behind a set of drums. I feel a strength of confidence and control in my natural abilities there. For, on the drums, I bridge the gap between my heartfelt gut or instinct, and the sound produced. I don't have to think music or mathematics anymore. Twenty-five years of practice and rudiments have brought me past that. Now, if I hear it in my head, I can play it without having to check it through technically.

That's where one truly becomes an artist. I'm pleased with what I have chosen as a profession. Notwithstanding I have always found it amusing how people want to know a musician's opinion on a broad range of unrelated subjects, from politics to his favorite color, like on the cover of The Monkees or The Dave Clark Five albums.

If I were the best computer programmer in the world, or the fastest typist on the face of the earth, no one would give a damn about my opinion on anything, except maybe typing.

On the other hand, I sure am glad that music is not like the Olympics: the "Hundred Yard Paradiddle," for surely, having learned in New York City where egomaniac musicians have to check themselves, there is always someone — one block down or seven flights up — who is not only better than you, but much better.

Anyway, a true musician can never be totally satisfied lest he become stagnant, and reach no farther. A satisfied musician is dead to creatively, musically, explore and improve, and ends up in a rut until the satisfaction gives way to complacency, then frustration forces one to reach for something. Something unknown. Something one knows when he finds it. Something new! No matter how many people tell you how good you are, if you're a true living artist, you don't believe it. By my definition, you can't.

Another thing people don't consider is the farther you come, the harder the progress gets. The more improved one gets, the less room for improvement there literally is. When the field narrows, the artists who got into it for the trappings as a goal fades, and the ones who were driven from purer source — like just loving an instrument — will weather the doldrums of playing through the rut of satisfaction.

Back to Europe where our next stop is Amsterdam. Ahh, Amsterdam... Hash bars, and a Red-Light District, where the prostitutes actually hang out in storefront windows with red lights and advertise their wares. Some of them are quite beautiful in their lingerie and leather. They look like mannequins from Frederick's of Hollywood.

We were taken by the charm of hash bars like The Bulldog, The Grasshopper, and the Mustang Hauf. The Mustang Hauf had a couple of small rooms upstairs for those who needed to sleep their smoke off. We walked in with a couple of locals. They walked over to the counter and asked for a menu. A MENU?!?!

Man, I could scarcely believe it. "And what's on this little menu?" you ask. Oh, things as tasty as Nepalese blonde, Afghanistan red, black opiated, and a couple of kinds of super-weed Dutch Skunk and some others, and prices next to the description. Most of the prices ranged about twenty-five guilders. Some things you must see to appreciate. The shops are called "coffee houses." They almost all have the Rasta colors of orange, green, and yellow in their sign, or in their window.

They were spotlessly clean, and above board. They served a few different coffees, and fresh squeezed juice, and muffins and stuff. They just sold pot and hash also! It was all so damn civilized. We loved it!

Amsterdam has always been one of my favorite cities for several reasons. Everyone speaks English; that's one thing that's bound to make you feel more at home. The bicycles, the food, and the relaxed good life that people in the Netherlands seem to enjoy, unlike the uptight Germans. However, it also means no all-night, on-the-edge, frantic Berlin. Amsterdam makes me think of San Francisco, my home, and it does have Coffee Houses!

We were playing the famous Paradiso. It's the place to play in town. Everyone from the Rolling Stones to the Grateful Dead have played there. A cool building with a cool history. We were backstage, which here meant downstairs under the dance floor. It's getting near show time when all of a sudden, we hear this thudding sound. In threes, like "thud-thud-thud," rest and repeat.

It's coming from upstairs, and it's getting louder, our dressing room door opens, I can now hear the muted sound of voices in unison with the curious drum beat. It's chanting, "MDC!" Huh?

I thought, "MDC." It is, they are, "MDC!" The door opens again. It is Biafra. Biafra says, "Well, it looks like you guys are going to blow us away tonight." I got hit with a small piece of plaster from the ceiling. I looked at Klaus, saying, "Tonight, he may be right!"

We took the stage amidst the shrill cheers that sounded like crickets, the biggest reaction we had ever had. We looked at one another, thinking, "Really? For us!"

It was for us. We were later to find out that Hank Schmidt, owner of four or five major underground record stores in Holland, loved our album, and when people came to get the hopelessly delayed Kennedys' record, he would tell them that it wasn't out yet, but this was the new hot-shit disk from America, these guys are playing with the DKs. He sold hundreds in Amsterdam alone. He instructed the other stores to do the same. By the time we played there, we had sold more vinyl in Holland than we had in the whole of Great Britain.

People of Holland loved it, and bought it, and the happy result was cheering pandemonium at the Paradiso. Word spreads quickly in a place like Holland, and we owe the thrill of that welcome on stage to Hank.

There were eighteen shows in all in Europe with the DKs. All of them were well attended, and all were successful. *Plastic Surgery Disasters*, the Kennedys' record, didn't come out after their departure. This was a shame, and a financial disaster. The sales lost, when the iron was hot but the product unavailable, are seldom ever regained. I feel with all the extra problems and heartache this caused, we wound up being an additional burden to them, and put extra pressure on Biafra. For that, I'll always feel regret.

It was the first of eight times we would tour Europe (so far), and it was the Dead Kennedys' last. It would be the end of an era in punk. One of the true giants of the genre would never achieve the same glory again.

MDC always will be grateful to Biafra, Ray, Klaus, and Darren Peligro for sharing those shows. They gave us Europe, and I'll never forget.

94

12

I was the first of us to return to San Francisco. When I got back, I was surprised to find a telegram. Along with it was a magazine. It was big and shiny, a slick production. It was the summer edition of the Yippies' periodical, *Overthrow*.

This would have been of marginal interest, except the back cover, and I mean, the whole back cover, was a picture of the back of our album, proclaiming in large type, "Album of the Year!"

They were setting up a fifty-city tour, and wanted us to play as much of it as we wanted. The charm that this tour offered was the nature of the venues. The state capital building in Madison, Wisconsin; the Boston Commons; Ann Arbor, Michigan for the annual Hash Bash. The bandshell in Central Park; playing while being towed up Fifth Avenue on a flatbed truck, from Washington Square Park on 14th Street, to the United Nations building on 41st, where we continued to play. (Fifth Avenue is a one way going down!) And, the crème de la crème: the Congressional Mall in front of the Lincoln Memorial on the Fourth of July, to name a few.

They invited us to play as many as we were willing to do. I called them back, and told them that I was only one vote, but I was excited to do at least a bunch of the shows. My late father was the biggest Civil War buff around. I knew my father wouldn't have liked what I was doing with my life, but he died when I was 15. So I always figured that I would never gain his approval for playing what we played. But he adored Abe, and this gig would be as close to his approval as I could get. Sometimes, you get to fill needs that you don't even know you had. It made the Lincoln Memorial gig almost an obsession. The other gigs were cool, but this one was for DAD!

It was surely a trick to convince my weary comrades to venture forth on still another leg of what seemed like an endless journey, suitable for a book by Homer or Pasternak.

It didn't take long to secure the blessing of our crew for the Fourth of July with Abe, but I was surprised that we signed on for the whole deal. I think when the Yippies decided to allow us to choose the other bands that we would be sharing the bills with, it became far more exciting. We, of course, picked all our favorite bands that were willing: The Dicks, The Crucifucks, DRI, and many others were to fill these bills culminating with the Fourth of July bash, with all the aforementioned bands plus Toxic Reasons, and, I'm pleased to say, our old tour brothers, Dead Kennedys.

It was only a few weeks between our return to SF, and when we had to leave on this RAR (Rock Against Reagan) tour. We were enjoying this little sabbatical, when here come Ron and Franco back to the Vats with a juicer. Not just any old juicer, but an Acme, fancy, stainless steel juicer, complete with "citrus attachments," and a price tag of $295! This was a hell of an expenditure for some broke schnooks making aces out of eights, especially without the consensus of the whole band.

"It's for all of our health," they said. "We need it to supplement our vegetarian diets, especially on the road!" It caused a row, but in the end, we all were okay with it. We even added to our contract rider, that, along with the obligatory case of soda and one of beer, we needed a 25-pound bag of carrots for juicing! One promoter said he thought that we were coming in a covered wagon, and needed the carrots for our horses.

So, to further the cause of good health, the new "wiser, healthier" MDC is on its mission from God, and stopped by the Rainbow Grocery in the Mission for supplies. These consisted of a large bag of spirulina (a dried algae, really healthy, tasted god-awful); a jug of hot sauce; chips; carrots; and of course, we had the Acme Juicer. Supplies in hand, our little rag tag Ford van braved still one more endless highway.

On to Michigan to join forces with the Yippies and hippies and other assorted tie-dyed assholes, laden with cheap funk pot, and a ten-ton sack of fucking lentils, in a wagon-train of buses and vans and cars, looking much like Mad Max Does Woodstock.

Everyone proceeded to start eating a concoction of hot sauce and spirulina on chips that, even to me, tasted pretty good. We washed it all down with carrot juice. Now, I like carrot juice, but these geniuses were drinking it like water. The concoction became their main staple, as well. I warned, "Don't change your diet so radically. Do it gradually, so your system can adjust," but what did I know? I was the dope fiend that they just put up with. Lisa, our equipment manager, was the first to get sick. Still, they kept on with the carrot juice every day. Franco had read a book by Victorus Lavinscus, a leading dietitian, and armed with this man's book, now knew everything.

One day I'm hanging with Spike from DRI, and he asked me, "Hey, Al, what's up with your band?"

"Whaddaya mean?" I replied.

"Look at 'em. They're all orange!" They were standing in front of the green DRI van, and, sure enough, my band was glowing orange. Spike knew of the carrot juice, as his band had opted for beer. He, their drummer Eric, and I looked at them, looked at each other, and started breaking up laughing. They never did figure out what was so funny.

Later on that tour, when we were holed up somewhere in the Midwest, Franco made an appointment to meet Victorus, his food guru, who had a farm in the area. I chose to stay behind, drink beer, and kick back with the Dicks and DRI. When they returned, they had found out that some of us were feeling sick because… Guess what?… You should always gradually change your diet. Why? you ask… So your system can adjust.

Well, whaddaya know? I only found out what Victorus had said

because of Dave's sense of fair play. Obviously, this piece of information would have gone unrelated to me by Franco or Ron. This would
mean that they were wrong, and even worse, I was right!

It was when the rest of my band left to visit that farm while I hung
out with everyone else, that I realized we were missing a lot of fun by
being pious. I mentioned this to Dave, who already seemed to have
figured that out. It hadn't been Dave being judgmental, anyhow. It
wasn't anyone, or anything in particular. The Victorus experience had
served to remind us that we were fallible, and that carrot juice, as well
as beer, are both thicker than water.

Armed with this updated, improved information, we now made
orange, apple, banana, and strawberry juices, as well as carrot juice.
With this assortment of flavors to choose from, and the variety of
combinations possible, I came to enjoy our investment as much as
anyone else.

Meanwhile back at Quentin... In their ceaseless search for
entertainment for their guests, the California Department of
Corrections, in association with the California Superior Court system,
is providing, at great expense, and with the whole-hearted blessing of
Governor Pete Wilson... AN EXECUTION!

Mr. W assures the public their production will be second to none.
And, of course, Keith Daniel Williams, the horse, dances the waltz.
This will certainly be Mr. Williams' last day without pay. He might
not lose his bitch, but he's surely lost all his turns. Brutal bastard, I
couldn't even imagine waiting for an asshole like Wilson, governor of
California, to call in a stay of execution. No, I'm sure that old Pete will
sleep well tonight, unless he's troubled again with creative ways to cut
more money from welfare mothers.

For those who don't know, Governor Pete Wilson is the creep
who, upon cutting money from the already meager AFDC (Aid for
Families with Dependent Children) told the objecting mothers that
they wouldn't be able to have that six-pack of beer.

Due to the media-heightened circus — the day before, which is today, and the day after, Saturday — have us celebrating by lounging around the old cell on lockdown. And guess what day our yard day is... yes, Saturday! Well, they wouldn't want us to keel over from too much fresh air. What was that big yellow thing in the sky called again, anyway? "Little darling, it's been a long, cold, lonely lockdown."

As brother Williams suddenly expires, an amazing thing happens. It started when a character named Funny Money, who was in for forgery and defacing money — making funny money, what else? — began telling hilarious tales about his adventures and misadventures. Before you know it, he's talking about how pained he is about the youngsters whom he can't tell not to make the same mistakes that he did. (Okay, he didn't say "whom.") This struck a chord in me, and some others, too.

Soon we're having a college-level, multi-tier, multi-race discussion that sounded like a graduate school forum. It covered legal, social, political, psychological, and sociological matters. All the "muthafuckers" and "bitches and ho's" disappeared, and insight, and love of family, and concern for the future, and dreams blossomed forth. It was the most profound hour I had spent since I arrived incarcerated.

Earlier this evening, my celly Chris and I went on our first "fishing" expedition. Our impossible mission, should we choose to accept it, was to get a book from our cell, number 1w 28, five tiers up to cell number 5w 21, and vice versa. All the tiers overhang one another, so this little maneuver involved a multi-cell, multi-tier effort. Pipes, and other fish lines — not to mention, literary sharks who might have a case of librario hijackus on their minds — all lay in our path. We had come into the deal with an always-valuable Sydney Sheldon... *Bloodline*, to be exact. The folks upstairs had an equally coveted *Rock Star* by Jackie Collins.

First, 5w 21 sent down a bed-sheet fishline with a copy of the *Title 15* as a sinker. The *Title 15* is the book of prison rules and regulations, and the consequences involved in disobeying them, among other delightful things. Things like a form for "Manner of Death Sentence Executions"... Gee whiz, poison gas or lethal injection? And they say that you don't have choices here in the pen! When we established that the line was in our sight, they hauled it back up, or should I say, "reeled it in." Then they attached the Collins. I think the authors of these books would smile to see the lengths that prisoners go to in obtaining their works.

The line came back down, but over all the tiers. They couldn't get it to swing in towards the bars enough for us to grab it. The cell one tier above ours, 2w 28, housed an experienced fisherman in his own right, and he came to our rescue. He lassoed the limp line and reeled it in, allowing it to hang closer. Pulling up and down from the railing on the fifth tier caused it to start to swing. Closer and closer it came. My skinny little arm was able to squeeze, at an angle, through the bars as slowly, gently, the Collins came closer.

It was just inches away now... steady, steady... My fingers tipped it, when... Oh no! Keys coming. Man walking. 5-0 on the tier! Damn! Fucking corrections officer. You can always find a pig when you don't want one.

"Haul it up," we yelled; fishing being one of those rules outlined in the *Title 15*, and up it went.

When the meddlesome guard (filthy screws) disappeared, I checked up and down the tier with my reflective fingernail clippers. After determining that the coast was as clear as it was going to get, we tried again.

This time, 2w 28's line got tangled in the water pipes right out of our reach. It broke when he tried to shake it loose. It seemed all was lost. The normal tier tenders, privileged prisoners known as "trusties," were all on lockdown due to the execution.

But, what was this? Some trusties, having indispensable tasks, were free. Most of them were in the kitchen. Most of them, but not all... for one of them was walking right on by! This welcome visitor ripped the caught line free, and returned it to 2w 28. We were back in business again.

This time, 2w 28 caught and pulled in the fifth tier's line cleanly.

He then swung it in, and let it go just at the right moment. The *Title 15*, with the Collins attached, made it just into my grasp. We had our book. We attached the Sheldon to the line next to the rule book, and they hauled it back up.

I sit here now, Dear Reader, happy to not have to tell you about the one that got way.

13

Somewhere on the Rock Against Reagan excursion, I got a true sense of dread. It's the ultimate nightmare, something that only happens to John Candy in the movies. We are in Ohio somewhere, "we" being the RAR caravan, consisting of — as I might have mentioned — three Dayglo buses that scream, SEARCH ME! SEARCH ME! LOOK AT MY PAINT JOB, I GOTTA HAVE DRUGS! and a Ryder box truck that carried the equipment, and about a dozen other vehicles: band vans, private cars, and whatnot. I, as had been my habit, was traveling in a number of vehicles. For this stretch, I happened to be traveling in the DRI van.

I go to catch up on my reading in the little boys' room. I was not gone for more than ten minutes, but when I emerged, to my horror, the parking lot was empty! I had been left behind by every vehicle, one thinking that I was in another. GODDAMN IT, NOBODY EVEN KNEW I WAS MISSING!!!

Of course, I had no money, and was literally up the river in the middle of nowhere without a canoe, much less a paddle. I didn't even know exactly where they were headed, except the city. No idea who to call. No money. Suddenly, the miserable lentil hippie soup sounded pretty good. Totally in denial of what had just transpired, I walked numbly to the corner and sat down.

Suddenly, I had a thought! Naw, it's too much of a long shot... With nothing more pressing to inquire about, I asked, "Is there a health food store in the town just ahead?" The gas station people shrugged, but by consulting a phone book, we found there was.

Unbelievable! My predictable companions had chosen that time to replenish their supplies. I almost cried when Franco got on the phone. As I might have mentioned, Franco used to paraphrase the Blues Brothers movie, saying, "We're on a mission from God." Anyway, someone was looking out for my sorry punk rock butt that day, for sure.

A week or so later, we're playing the famous Boston Commons. As usual, the Yippies were running way behind schedule. The sound permit was not flexible, and the sound WAS going to end at five. This fact became increasingly apparent by the gradual closing in by the police. The Dicks took the stage, (that is, the band "The Dicks," not the cops). DRI and MDC hadn't played yet. The Dicks played an inspired twenty-minute set ending with "Dicks Hate the Police." Then the fastest set change I've ever been witness to happened. Amps and drums changed like wheels on an Indy racecar. The same David Copperfield-like disappearing act flashed its way to change MDC into DRI. "Hey, Rocky! Watch me pull a Dead Cop out of my hat!" Two complete backline changeovers in less than five minutes! The slow as molasses Yippies almost had a stroke. Sure as hell, the Boston Police yanked the cord at 5:01pm.

The Boston pigs are also called MDC: Municipal District Constabulary. I always thought that word "constabulary" had an appropriate sound: CON STAB U in the back LARY. (Enough already, Al.)

Although abbreviated sets were played all around, still Beantown got its dose of western, if not West Coast, hardcore, and the Boston baked backstabbers, or whomever, did not get the satisfaction of nixing any of us out.

In the future, I was to relate this story to bands at times when backstage laziness was going to fuck with our show. Often, the nice guy was to be found playing Garcia riffs on Haight Street, certainly not behind the unfriendly drums of MDC, especially a late MDC. I know it sounds like Mr. Pissy and his rock star pretend-world of amps that go to eleven.

In fact, it has nothing to do with anything more than the buses leave when they leave. There is always a shank of the evening: play much after that, and the effort is expended to a thinned-out audience with the next day's obligations having taken their toll. Even the ones who remain have been worn by the barrage of volume and the lateness of the hour. So I will remain famous (and infamous) for rushing equipment changes. For this, I wish to extend my personal no apology.

At this point, I think it's germane to mention that I was the equipment manager for years, back at the beginning. Back then, MDC divided up the numerous band responsibilities. For example, I did the equipment. Doing the equipment meant (and still does mean) overseeing the moving and maintenance of all the equipment. That is not to say that I single-handedly moved everything. No, on tour, it's more like grab a big, strong, punk rock local, and maybe his friends, and see if you can get him, or them, to do all of the moving in exchange for a t-shirt or two. It did mean that you didn't get to "punch out" and belly up to the bar, in a Dave Dictorly fashion right off the stage. Ron Posner, our guitarist, maintained the finances and took care of the van. He was perfect with the money because of his... I'd like to say "frugal" but "cheap" was more like it. (Bless yer penny-pinching heart, Ron!) He also wrote most of the raw musical themes that were to become our best loved record, *Millions of Dead Cops*.

Franco did the phone work, and much of the negotiations. I'm sad to say this was to our detriment much of the time. Without being any bloodier than necessary, the misuse of this responsibility was the undoing of our label, R. Radical Records, and eventually was the undoing of Franco as MDC's bass player himself. If we knew then what we know now, we probably would still have the record label, like many other bands whose record businesses outlasted even their groups. If, if, if. If my aunt had balls, she'd have been my uncle... (Relevance, Al, relevance!)

Dave did (and still does to this day) the mail order and other mail. These band responsibilities just seemed to evolve naturally. As we went on, when needs arose, the most naturally qualified (or available) hands took them on. We were a 24/7 band with serious intent. The music, fortunately was a shared responsibility. We all contributed. Ron wrote the most music, or at least the most difficult progressions and themes. Dave had written most of the words, and I bridged the gap. I think we owe a good deal of our musical success to the fact that, unlike most bands, no one member of the band did all, or even the lion's share, of the composing.

Our musical backgrounds were diverse as well. Ron had come from Venezuela. He could play flamenco and other Spanish guitar styles "like ringing a bell," as Mr. Berry would put it. MDC, incredibly, was his first band, and his first experience with electric guitar. I brought to the table a varied style honed on somewhat rock and blues, but mostly weaned on jazz. I also prided myself on being able to play fluently in almost any time signature.

At first, Ron wrote in four-four time exclusively. As you can hear on our records, many things were altered from that rhythm, winding up in five-four or seven-eight time. This was usually my contribution. Although Ron and I didn't like each other much on a personal level, we had one thing in common: we both loved MDC and the way each other played. So, if I were to bring up a change in the music, I always tried to make absolutely sure that the change was a definite improvement, not just a self-indulgent complication. To that end, I would work through any change in every way I heard it, so that I would've not only made sure that the change was called for, but definitely an improvement and the tastiest approach. I dreaded the day that Ron would lose enthusiasm for my ideas. Happy to say he never did. I suppose one doesn't necessarily have to be a good guy to have good taste.

While painfully splitting hairs in LA one afternoon over what credits were appropriate for which songs on our first album, we decided to settle much the same as Lennon-McCartney had. We just published the whole shebang as "words and music by MDC." Again, this was mostly a concession to Franco, who attempted to snake his name onto songs he had nothing do with. The rational was supposed to make us the four musketeers, but we really were, in retrospect, the four stooges. "One for all, and All for none!"

PAGING MR. SCHVITZ! PLEASE RETURN TO THE FUCKIN' STORY...

MDC finally made it down to New York City where we checked into number 9 Bleeker Street in the Village, the main headquarters of the Yippies. What information we had about the Yippies and their finances were later confirmed at number 9. This was that this RAR tour was all a way to spend the profits of the year's marijuana business. We, being avid users of quality herbs, could deal with this reality.

After all, a few days later, we would be strapped down on a flatbed truck being hauled UP Fifth Avenue, a major one-way street that, when open, flows the opposite direction downtown. Now the upper crust East Side would have MDC to deal with! As we rocked, rolled, and brutally thrashed through a bunch of anti-rich and your basic "Business on Parade"-oriented set, we were being pulled right past the most exclusive stores in the world: Tiffany, Gucci, and the original Saks Fifth Ave. Dave was at his most brilliant, ad-libbing tailor-made comments at the horrified shoppers in between the songs.

"Hey, you, in the mink!" or "Hey there, with your French poodle! How much blood was spilled to satisfy your desire for a piece of flesh on your fork, or on your back ,or that fancy fur collar 'round your death-ridden coat?"

Onward up Fifth to 41st Street, an acoustic nightmare, if there ever was one. We would be playing directly at a building, and the instant reverberation made the drums play themselves. It would sound full and rich but much too boomy. As we'd progress on down the avenue, different building with different surfaces and dimensions caused constant change. Sometimes the mids would smack you in the face. Other times I couldn't hear anything but bass. The most amazing effect occurred when we would pass a cross street. The sound would be full as an indoor nightclub until the second we hit the cross street, then it would disappear. All that was left was a thin guitar and wimpy-sounding drums. It felt to me like we were being sucked up with sound, a compelling, unseen force like an auditory undertow, pulling us along with the sound. Then a few seconds later, when we reached the other side of the intersection, *Boom!* The sound would snap back as abruptly and forcefully as it had left.

Although we traveled from 14th Street, all the way up to 41st Street, passing at least thirty intersections, I never got used to that vacuum cleaner effect sucking all the life out of our musical souls.

We turned right at 41st Street, straight down to the base of the United Nations building. It was all a unique experience I'll never forget. Life was good. MDC was alive and well, and for a time it seemed, at least by the quality of venues, that we were on the upward swing. Onward, and full steam ahead! Lincoln Memorial or bust.

This road would not be without difficulties. Constant vehicular problems, equipment malfunctions, and, of course, the occasional bust. Communication breakdowns between the local Yippies and the national tour Yippies, and/or the local promoters, were common. The money from Yip Central at 9 Bleeker Street was always behind, and often short. MDC, fortunately, could fill in empty dates with well-paying shows that helped us keep our heads above water. At least, naturally, there was plenty of juice around when we were around.

14

ONE MONTH DOWN, ETERNITY TO GO... four weeks to the day, today. At 5 o'clock in the morning this morning, my celly unexpectedly moved out. He had to go back to Solano County for a trial. So today I'm left completely alone. Funny, but I'm feeling lonesome. Now for West Block, I'm well set up. I brought 150 envelopes. That is the maximum amount they'll allow you to bring. Envelopes are the currency one must use until one "goes to the store." Having prepared for this monetary situation, I wasn't in need of anything. Anything that is to be had in prison reception's West Block, that is. I paid off the canteen clerk with two cans of tuna in order to get to the store at the first availability. Now I had not only tobacco, and hot coffee, and hot chocolate, ramen-type soups, and other stuff, but I also was blessed with writing paper, as this account shows. Well, my entrepreneurial skills have carried over the wall to the inside. I've not only stocked myself fat, but actually made all my envelopes back.

I received my first two pieces of mail yesterday. One was a return of a letter that I'd sent out with an incomplete address, meaning I didn't have the whole zip code. Christ, the fucking thing was going to Haight Street in San Francisco. What the fuck? The other was a letter from my friend, Gene. I'm kind of worried about my mom because I know that she's written me, and I worry about what toll this whole experience is having on her.

I expect that they'll move me from my deluxe single room with a view of the wall, or at least pack another " 'wood" in here with me, sooner than later. Anyway, on the odd week when the canteen is closed, I'm about the "fattest" man in town. I'm down enough though, that I had to cut out the Mother Teresa trip I was doing lest I be begging for "snipes" (cigarette butts) myself. People around here are giving up their whole lunch for one cigarette. Life is hard in West Block, but 1W 28 has it goin' on!

I have some folks from the county jail at San Bruno to thank. They told me about the envelopes, and other key information about prison etiquette. There are many things to know about the do's and don'ts of the pen, things that can get you through and things that can get you killed. One of these folks was Paulie M. He's an OG from way back. He used to scare the hell out of me with his prison tales. I could also tell that the stories were true. However, if the particulars of, let's say, "The Telltale Heart" were clinically described, police report style, it surely would not have the same chilling effect. Well, Paulie was perhaps not Edgar Allen Poe, but with the real-life stories like Quentin has to offer, "chilling" was just the word. Although Paulie enjoyed the terror he was putting me through, it served to make me sit back, and watch, and listen. I knew who was behind me at any given time. I already knew what "dry snitching" was all about. I knew what SPPS was… What? you want me to tell you? No thanks… Yes, above all, you learned to mind your own business.

Anyway, Paulie shows up about a week ago. A bad turn of luck in the courtroom, and six months in County becomes sixteen months in the pen. Whadda state, California… Anyway, the first time we run into each other was in the chow hall. There he is, with a "boy, am I glad to see you" grin on his face. He was never that glad to see me in the County. I was just as pleased to be able to tighten him up with tobacco in the middle of the odd week drought.

I've been reading like a fiend in here, and have been extremely lucky to have a fairly steady supply of good books. It is one way out of here, albeit temporary, at best. I also have been able to obtain some unheard-of items in here, namely a chess set and a set of dominos. So "it's on" in old 1w 28.

Yesterday being laundry day, I have a huge supply of t-shirts, shorts, and socks. I even bought a combination lock to protect my coveted items during chow, showers, and yard.

In West Block, there is no access to the phone, except for the tier workers. The only source of information is the mail. I wish I'd get a letter from my mom or my kids to put my mind at ease. I'm sure everyone is fine, but still mail is one of the few luxuries allowed in West Block.

On the other hand, ...THEY'VE GOT SHOWERS! Did you say showers? Man, they got 'em here, and how! And guess what? You get to share them with fifty or more burly men. Today, just for a special surprise treat, no hot water! Try to imagine the scene, Dear Reader: one thousand grown men dashing through, soaping up, shivering, shriveling, fifty at a time, then bailing back to their cells with teeth a-chatter. No pretty sight, I assure you. Book your reservations now. Governor Wilson has plans to fill up many more of these intimate hygiene accommodations before the end of the century.

I do have something to brag about though. It happened before I could do anything about it, almost before I saw it. I am feeling particularly pampered with my brand-new bar of Irish Spring soap. I've been forced to use the rough, nasty state soap for a month. But what now?! Yikes! My soap is doing a gentle end-over-end flip as it flies out of my hand. FUCK ME! It's like what they say about your life flashing before your eyes before you die. Well, in the ten nozzle-head shower at Quentin, it's much the same thing when you look down, and to your horror, surrounded by three pairs of feet, there it is MY SOAP! I looked at a group of guys grinning at me, wondering what I was going to next. So did I!

"Well, fuck this!" I growled in my most ominous, gravelly, prison-type voice, and then bent at the knees, and grabbed my soap, while everyone in the shower had a good laugh on me!

I was to hear that tale told on the yard for a week. Moments that funny are important in the pen. So, Dear Reader, I am one of the people who can say, "I dropped the soap in the shower at old San Quentin," and not only lived to tell the tale, but remained a virgin.

Actually, I must confess to giving up my virginity to a large, uncomfortable test-tube full of meth when flying into Frankfurt, Germany, but that's another story.

13

"See the new cell? Same as the old cell. Oh, well." This morning I awoke to a cell move. They moved me to Badger section. Badger section looks just the same as West Block. It's just another part of the reception system at Quentin. I didn't write anything yesterday because I was kind of depressed, and when that happens, I lose my sense of humor.

This I can't allow. It's my strongest connection with my sanity, not to mention my humanity. When I miss my children, and friends, and my mischievous Miss Mayginn, I tell myself that it's just a mood, and like time itself, time being my major enemy, WILL pass. Soon, as I knew it would, my sadness did so pass. So, I'm back!

It's a bit past noon here in B Section, and I'm on the Bay side where I can glimpse a slice of the San Francisco Bay. At first, it seemed nice, but then when I could see the Larkspur Ferry shuttling free people away from here three times a day, it wasn't making my time go any quicker. So, fuck that barge. It has given us a new tradition though. When the loaded ferry shows up, some satanic, tone deaf choir boy sings *The Love Boat* theme. Boy, if Jack Jones ever heard this, he'd jump ship!

I'm now on the third tier, and the guard (filthy screw, you'll never take me alive, copper!) armed with an M-14 walks the catwalk right across from me. In addition to the close-set bars, there is a black grid of tight little triangles. This makes the tiny cell as dark as it is small. It doesn't do much for your disposition either. In my depression, I asked my celly, Ben, what the deal was with these miserable gratings welded to our bars. He told me that late in the '60s some convict, in a moment of inspiration, fashioned himself a handy, dandy little "shank." (Dat's whatyas calls a shiv in da joint.) He then sat back in delicious anticipation. Soon the moment of glory had arrived. As the unsuspecting prey approached, he reached out, and stabs the cop. First in the side, then in the stomach, where he gives the blade a friendly twist for emphasis. One more slash to the neck and there you have it! Look, up in the sky… It's a bird… It's a plane! No, it's a fucking CO gracefully falling to his death over the fifth tier railing!

Bravo! Well done! In honor of this hero and his inspired deed, the huge grids were permanently welded to the original design; a vote of "thanks" to the brave convict to which all convicts owe a debt of gratitude. Thanks.

So, as I look at the mesh fitted door of bars on my cage, I smile and know it represents the fear that the correction officers around here have of the inmates, us convicts. After all, they had better watch out for me… I sold a bag of dope!

In all deadly seriousness, however, there are other enemies in here. Upon occasion, the armed scum in the towers and on the catwalks are even reassuring, as strange as that might sound. In large red letters, right across from me is a sign. It reads: NO WARNING SHOTS FIRED IN THIS UNIT! Now, if you're thinking that they mean they won't shoot in here, you'd be wrong… dead wrong, perhaps.

No, the other interpretation is the real deal. I govern myself with a credo of vigilance. Always know who is behind you and, never go anywhere alone. One doesn't ever talk to any guard without another convict present, lest you be seen and misconstrued as a snitch. One must be careful of having someone put a "jacket" on you. In prison, you watch what you say, and to whom you say it. The wrong comment said around the wrong person, and you could find yourself flying after that CO off the tier down to your death. And, should you see something, you didn't see nothing. The etiquette in prison is clear.

I'm short. Meaning that I get out relatively soon. This is something you keep to yourself. Jealousy can also be a deadly excuse to someone with nothing to lose, no light at the end of an endless tunnel. I refrain from comment, and avoid getting into anyone else's mix as much as possible. I'm here doing my time, and want no part of anybody else's.

As Funny Money would put it, "They ain't playing, and if they is, they playing for keeps!"

Another fear is having a fucked-up celly. You don't get to choose your partner for this little dance. In this department, I have been extremely lucky. My first celly, Chris, was a real nice guy (and I'm sure still is). He was stressed a bit, but that's to be expected since he got a harsh sentence. We played a bunch of chess and dominos, and he was teaching me Pinochle.

My next celly, who'll remain nameless lest I run into him in the future, was a pig who coughed, and farted, and whined the entire two days we were celled up together. Thank god, I was moved to Badger section after that.

My third celly, and the one I'd be with the rest of my stay, was Ben. Ben was the type who, like me, had no interest in anyone else's game. He was the guy with the historical information on the grating outside our cells.

Your celly can make your hard time harder. I shudder to think what life would have been if I had been stuck with Mr. TB Fartalot. But enough about me, Dear Reader. Let's talk about you. What do you think of me?! Sorry, old joke... but this book did take me a couple of decades to get published. I believe I was telling you about the Fourth of July celebration at the Congressional Mall in DC...

The sky was cloudless on this Independence Day. It was 1983, and old Honest Abe is in attendance. He has an excellent view from backstage, and a comfortable chair to watch the whole spectacle. Punk rock has more or less dominated his corner of the mall. At the other end, toward the White House, Wayne Newton, and whatever manner of life form he attracts, are having a pleasant little outing.

So, there it is. The right-wing, conservative Republican New-tonites, and the radical, Reagan-hating — dare I say? — left. Left is the opposite of right, isn't it? Well, it is, down on the Lincoln end of the mall. The Newtonites would probably say that the opposite of right is wrong, to paraphrase Leon Russell.

The stage is mercifully covered, so the bands could play in the shade of the grueling heat. I watched DRI and Toxic Reasons play killer sets and practically pass out in the summer broil. From back-stage, I was pleased to see Lincoln in his huge chair. It seemed fitting to have our sixteenth president relaxed and seated some "six score and thirteen years" after Gettysburg.

The sun was thankfully going down by the time we played. From my perch on the drum riser, I could see the Jefferson Memorial and the Capitol building. Jefferson's back was towards me, which was fine. His slave-owning ass could stay away on Independence Day, as far as I was concerned. Across from me, as I squinted, was the Capitol, and in the middle, was the tall, pencil-like Washington Monument. I could barely see the top of old 1600 Pennsylvania Avenue, but I could prac-tically hear Reagan wallowing around in an Alzheimer's haze, think-ing, Which way did he go, George?, trying to remember what he was supposed to forget... "Was that Arms for Contras, or more money for General Noriega? Oh well, I think I'll slip in my tape of *Bedtime for Bonzo*, and take another nap. Tell Casey and Bush to run the store for me, would you please, Nancy?"

Our set went off without a hitch, and, after a reggae band, some politicos with their jargon about legalization of pot, it was time for Dead Kennedys. This would be the last time I would get to see them perform as a band, although I didn't know it then.

They took the stage at dusk. The first thing Biafra was to com-ment on was the monstrosity right in front of him, the Washington Monument. He described it (much more cleverly than I) as the Great Washington Klansman, which its pointed head and shape certainly did resemble, and referred to the blinking red lights at the windows on the top — there to prevent airplanes from crashing into it at night — as eyes winking to remind us that Washington himself had slaves.

This ad-lib characterization was brilliant and exactly on the money. A fifty-story Knight of the Ku Klux Klan. Again, my hat is off to one of the sharpest and most provocative minds in punk rock. The Kennedys then proceeded to play the most powerful set I'd ever seen them play.

Mr. Newton and his ilk, playing at the same time, did not escape the masterful wit of Biafra unscathed. No, Wayne and his Reaganite fans were raked over the coals as well. All and all, an inspiring day for Punk Rock.

We played our way back to San Francisco where we separated from one another for a well-deserved break. This break proved to be a permanent separation of the original line-up of MDC, forever.

16

"Maybe it was no one's fault, I know it wasn't mine," sayeth Ian MacKaye in the Minor Threat song "Betray." I think these are ultimately words of wisdom. I believe that the differences or at least issues weren't personal until a disagreement, a difference of opinion. And as in most personal issues, there is much blaming and denial.

We were hell-bent on drawing deep lines in the sand. We then personalized these lines into deep painful wounds, some of which would never heal. Somehow, I thought that we would fight and argue, particularly Ron and I, like two cantankerous old men, forever. I kind of thought that we were like *The Sunshine Boys*, a movie where Walter Matthau and George Burns played vaudevillians who always fought but "the show must go on!".

I also felt an indescribable sort of reverse psychological camaraderie with Ron. Oh, the way we could play together. Like a machine gun or a typewriter. I didn't realize it at the time, but we played so tightly because we resented each other, not because we liked each other or even loved the music. Which, at least, I did.

All these differences wouldn't have broken us up, as long as we still had more in common than we differed, and we had the greatest motivator of all, we were hungry! But the strain of touring and exhaustion added to the conglomeration of "baggage," both suppressed and spoken, was more than enough to scuttle the ship when it came down to whether or not we should go back to Europe. An enticing little offer was on the table. It involved gigs with Crass, and everything. This was, unfortunately, not what I had planned for the winter. I was caught by surprise and found that I was not only unenthusiastic by the prospect of another tour so soon, I was dreading it.

I decided that I didn't want to spend the winter with the same folks I shared everyday for the past two and a half years. It was no shock to me that this decision caused resentment with my bandmates, but I didn't think this was going to be the end of the original four members playing together again. I guess I was naive. I hadn't thought about what life would be like without being part of the band. I would be lying if I didn't admit that my first reaction to the band getting John Leib to replace me, at least for this tour, was relief. As I have said, I didn't anticipate the awkwardness I felt, in just dealing with people in general. I came to San Francisco a tenured original member of a fairly major Punk Rock band, and this was how people here viewed me. Now, some folks were different with all sorts of reactions. Had I known that the Vats that had been home to so many friends and musicians, was going to fall victim to the clean up for the Democratic Convention, that might have been a factor. But, I didn't know so I can't really say.

Cecilia and I were at the Vats for the fires set to empty the building so it could be demolished. At least that's is what we all assumed (the twenty or so bands and artists that lived and worked or practiced there). The first we thought was just an accident, but the second and scarier fire was too much. I was awoken by Kurt from DRI yelling down the pipe, "Hey, Al, it's another fire and this one's bad. GET OUT!"

We grabbed our stuff and fought thick smoke to get out. I went back in and rescued Cecilia's two cats that were frozen with fear. We were outside and I was taking inventory of the people to make sure everyone was accounted for when I realized that we had two friends who lived in the upstairs office who were missing! I yelled up as loud as I could to the fifth floor window until our friend Eric stuck his head out. Eric and Jerry were dead asleep and barely made it out through the smoke. Eric told me that they probably wouldn't have made it out if I hadn't called up to them. Nobody thought of them in the office in the back. The fire itself wasn't what one would die from. The smoke, thick and black and caused by the Ebonite rubberized vat walls, would kill you first. I got some serious hugs from both of those guys. I decided that alone made me glad I wasn't in Europe.

Cecilia and I found a little basement in an office building on an alley named Lusk that we rented and adapted for rehearsal space and living quarters. That's not "lust" or "dusk", just Lusk! We put walls up and rented to two other bands as well. We even had a show there once. It just happened to be "Poison Idea" complete with the legendary Tom Pig Champion.

17

In the blackness of January 1984, two beacons showed me light, mercy, and salvation. One was The White Lie, and the other being China Swartz. China was my bright new love, and a year later became the mother of my first son, Brian.

The White Lie was a brand-new collaboration with the single most talented musician that it has ever been my privilege and certainly my pleasure to work with. That would be Barry D'alive. The White Lie was actually the second musical project in which I became involved with during this break from MDC. I did, for a short while, play with the Pop-o-Pies. Joe Pie enticed me into joining up by telling me about a show they had booked on New Year's Eve at Winterland, opening for the Grateful Dead. Well, I certainly could be coerced into such a gig, notwithstanding the proper touché! Playing that show would certainly be a needed feather in my cap bigtime!

Unfortunately, somehow, we lost the show. I was way pissed. It did help to find out that The Band reformed to be the opener for that New Year's show. Bumped by, or for, the best. We did, however, book a show at Ruthie's Inn in Berkeley, opening for Flipper, which was a blast, and I owe it to Joe Pie for reviving my interest in playing. The creation of The White Lie was soon to follow.

I came to know the too clever for his own good, musically gifted, hot shit guitar and bass playing, quick witted, wise cracking, Barry Ward D'alive when he came up from Houston to replace Dennis on bass for DRI. Dennis, for some reason, couldn't hang and went home, leaving DRI high and … well, DRI. (Alright, pun intended.)

Barry was ousted from DRI due to one of the most bizarre set of circumstances I've ever heard. It seemed that Barry used to play for a Houston band called Stark Raving Mad. Steve, Stark Raving Mad's drummer, was married to a gal who also happened to be the sister of Spike, DRI's guitarist. When Barry left Stark Raving Mad, this caused a rift between Spike's family and Barry. One day Spike just comes up to Barry, who has pulled up roots and moved seventeen hundred miles to join DRI, and tells him that he's kicked out of DRI because Steve's causing trouble for Spike's sister.

This left Barry detached, and when the Vats closed, homeless. He hadn't yet developed the circle of friends that I had over time to hit up for places to stay. Well, between the two of us, a great deal of residual resentment festered. We took the negative energy and turned it positive by using it to power a new force. It didn't hurt to have a bit of the old eye-opener about to help the lubricate the flow. We did have our cuts at our former band members, respectively. One of these took the form of a cover song with changed lyrics. It's a DRI song off their first album. I don't remember the title but it goes "Who am I? DRI," then a lyrical blur, then another chorus. Our version went: "Who am I? Who wants to know and why… We're not MDC, we're not DRI. We're strictly straight edge… except when were high! Who are I? We'll shout it from the sky… we're MDCRI. We're MDCRI. The White Lie."

It wasn't long before we had a dozen of the best songs we, or at least, I, ever produced.

MDC had some bad blood with this record producer named David Ferguson. At this point, I didn't care. In fact, I was able to capitalize on that anti-MDC energy since I left the band. Having at least that much in common, Ferguson was the first call I made in search some P&D (pressing and distribution) support. When we had twelve great songs ready, I called on David to come check out a rehearsal. His company was CD Records, and had to his credit the *Rat Music for Rat People, Volume I* record. That was the premier best punk compilation to date, and is my personal favorite of all time. Why not? It had all the best, or at least my favorite, bands on it. It had Flipper, Dead Kennedys, TSOL, Bad Brains, Black Flag, Circle Jerks, and a few I'm forgetting.

Now, David Ferguson had just compiled his second *Rat Music* album. It was another "Who's Who" of punk, including The Minutemen, Fang including Sammy, The Dicks, Personality Crisis, Tales of Terror, Butthole Surfers, and — yes — MDC and DRI! I wanted like hell to demonstrate that there was life after MDC, and could think of no better way than to have a competitive cut on that little smorgasbord of punk.

David told us regrettably that the *Rat* comp had already been mastered to disk, which would at least involved a remastering job. He was, however, impressed and excited by what he heard. I quickly got our brother-in-arms as far as the studio was concerned, Gary Creimann, to front us up some "trade time." Trade time is time that recording engineers get along with their pay, as a bonus or perquisite. They are not supposed to give or use trade time for paying customers, but I didn't fit that category anymore. Gary's always been a brother, and was glad to help me launch my new band in a major way on the *Rat* comp. You see, I told my band that if we worked hard and came up with slick tunes that I would see that we got on the *Rat Music* record. Unlike the other bands that recorded at Ferguson studio, we didn't have the time to take advantage of the studio that David owned part of, as it was booked well in advance. So, Gary was responsible for us having the chance to maybe get on a record that was already finished.

We recorded our first song that was especially designed not to be pro black or white or Jew or anything. It was an observation of a rather curious thing: that there should be a postcard stand at a Nazi death camp, with pictures of the ovens, prisoners — starving, half-dead people — much as if it were any other tourist attraction... "Greetings from the Most Horrifyingly Brutal and Inhumane Place in the Twentieth Century," or perhaps for the folks back home, "Dachau, Wish You Were Here!"

POSTCARD FROM DACHAU AlSchvitz

I got a line this morning, I should have stayed in bed.
A picture of an oven door, I thought of homemade bread.
Reminded me of cookies, when Mom dished out the chow
But this menu wasn't Kosher, the postcard was from DACHAU!

So who would you send this to, friends or family dear?
Saying "Hi, how are you?" or "Wish you were HERE!"
A picture of the ovens or a pile of corpses dead.
Or maybe for "best wishes," just prisoners underfed.

So I went over to Dachau to see it for myself
To the postcard stand where horror lined the shelf
And families with cameras posed on the oven doors
Joked and laughed like Nazis just before the war.

Chorus:
Postcard from Dachau, greetings from the war
Genocide full color, yours forevermore.
So Saturday at temple, you'll never be a bore
Just pass around the close-up of the crematory door!

The recording went well. We had recruited a fellow named Darren whom I had seen only once. I was at the Mab, checking out a band from the 'burbs called Three Mouse Guitars, when for only one or two songs a guest singer and dancer appeared. I have never seen any one person make such a difference. He single-handedly took these suburban-looking kids and made them into a severely directed, focused, powerful band. Darren is a black man with very strong features. He held the stage with a kind of… magnetism. I'd only known a few people with that extent of this kind of magic. Dave Dictor is one of those.

A band is like an energy-emitting source of sound. From a theatrical standpoint, the singer is like a prism reflecting and refracting the musical energy, much like light does in a glass prism. Darren took the rather thin-sounding TMG, and gave them stature. I had a vision. The Bad Brains had given black punk a bad name with all their religious prejudice and their thievery. A band with chops like ours, and the star quality and presence of Darren saying something, if not new, at least differently, than it had ever been done before.

Fucking A, we did it! I pressed David Ferguson to let us be on the comp. After all, we had paid for the recording. The re-mastering shouldn't be so expensive. I understand his not wanting to undo some work that he himself had considered done. After discussing the options, including the White Lie album, I made him see the financial logic that this record was not doing his label or his new premier band any favors leaving the "sure to be hometown fave" off his comp.

I couldn't resist trying to push my luck a bit. I always felt that the most important slots on a record, as far as the order (or sequence) is concerned, are the first and last cuts, the very first thing, or note, you hear, and the final sound resounding in your head. I opted for the final tone, due to the theatrical dynamic of the song we had chosen. You would have to hear it to know just what I mean. It's definitely an album-ending sort of coda. So, the second *Rat Music for Rat People* compilation ended with "Postcard from Dachau" by a band that at the time of the recording had played no gigs. A significant accomplishment.

M.D.C.
D.R.I. J.F.A.
DICKS FANG
MINUTEMEN BIG BOYS
THE WHITE LIE TALES OF TERROR
BUTTHOLE SURFERS PERSONALITY CRISIS

18

It seemed like minutes, but it was really months (though not more than four), when the Fire Commission decided that the basement on Lusk wasn't suitable for habitation and music, shut it down, and kicked us out. With nowhere to live, much less practice, the White Lie lost momentum. Two compilations and three shows: a short career. However, songs and parts of songs appear in later MDC records and RKL tunes.

Cecilia and I kind of drifted apart and I moved in with China, and, somehow, we managed to lose that apartment about a month later. We spent the next seven months homeless. MDC had returned home from Europe, but, with the exception of the Democratic National Convention held in San Francisco, played no more shows in 1984.

Had it not been for China, I would have given up hope of anything ever getting better. I really was at the lowest point of my life. We almost always found places to stay, but there were times when we slept in cars, and once, freezing, at the bottom of the stairs in the parking garage at Bush and Stockton Streets.

We'd always been pretty generous with our living accommodations when we were blessed enough to have them, so that helped at times, though I can remember being refused a night's flop for me and China by some people, or should I say "person"? You know who you are, Scumbag... I refuse to dignify your ability to have ever refused me anything by not mentioning your name herein, Fuckface, who I had allowed to sleep at my studio two or three times. Please forgive my self-indulgence, Dear Reader, I owed it to myself.

Then, out of nowhere, on a lucky fluke, I was staying at Franco's studio on Oakdale Avenue when Jayed Scotti, Biafra's roommate and artist, called to asked if we knew of anyone who was looking for a studio to share with his band The Feederz. "Yeah!" I said enthusiastically.

This was a week before Christmas, 1984. On January 1st, we moved in. China and I had a home. Nine months and twenty-three days later, I called Dave about four in the morning as he had told me to. I asked him to drive me to the Kaiser Permanente Hospital. It was time. He told me that I had better call a cab. I told him not to worry as I already had. By 8:30 a.m., I held the most beautiful little boy in my arms, and he was my son.

Most of the darkness that was 1984, and the leftover cobwebs, melted away. Things were looking up.

Things were not looking up for one of my fellow convicts back here in Quentin. It happened right in front of me, out in the yard. One inmate slashed another right across the throat. I saw the slashed inmate's eyes widen and mouth drop open in disbelief. He jumped back suddenly. The fast movement caught me by surprise. I didn't even know that anything was wrong until the blood… Oh, the blood. All over the front of his orange prison reception jumpsuit, spurting forth from his neck like a Wes Craven movie. I couldn't believe the guard. This guy was on his knees pouring blood and the guards made him lay down, flipped him over and cuffed him. He was high steppin' so not to bleed to death when they yanked him up to take him to the hospital. I didn't see the assailant, but even if I did, I didn't. My celly, Ben, was right next to me.

"Did you see that?" I asked.

He replied, "I didn't see nothin'," although I knew he had to have seen all I had. I knew from our angle that the assailant's back was to us, and he was gone before we even realized that anything had happened not to see.

I'll never forget the expression on the victim's face as he dropped his cigarettes and jumped back. Then whistles and sirens went off, and COs were everywhere.

"Time to sit down," Ben said. I'd learned to trust Ben's judgement, and immediately sat down on the ground. This occurred out in the yard, right after dinner. We sat and lay down on the ground while the COs walked around looking for the weapon. After not finding it, we all had to strip down to our shorts, and wait in three lines to be searched. As we waited in this "line of indignity," the buzzer goes off again. Some pig yells, "D block!" and twenty COs and two doctors rush into D. We were made to "Hit the ground" again. We never found out what was up in cell block D, but the whole affair certainly reminded me (as if I would ever forget) of the graveness of my new lodgings. After about two hours, we were allowed back into our cells.

Tomorrow was supposed to be yard but after this little altercation, I think it doubtful that we will get to go. The fun never stops here at good old Quentin. Damn, and I was looking so forward to getting out of this cell. This tiny, dark, depressing fucking cell.

Well, I'm over it, and wonder of all wonders, they did let us have yard. While we were out, a tour group of maybe twelve people escorted by two COs was led through, much as if Quentin were a zoo. It was depressing to hear the junior high locker room comments made by my fellow inmates about the female members of the tour group. Depressing, yes, but well, I looked at this heavyset, or big-boned — aah, fuck it! — this woman was fat, and had this smirk that said to me in a smug way, "Oh, you sex-starved bad men... so horny and inferior."

I commented loudly that this chick (a term I rarely use) could not take another bite from now until my release date and she'd still be fat! This caused some snickers, and wiped that smirk right off fatso's kisser... Then I saw a look of distain and disgust on another face.

"And that other one," I went on to challenge the glare. "My condition is temporary, I'll be out of in seven or eight months, but you'll be ugly forever!" That caused a bunch of laughter, and although I felt that

131

I betrayed myself on one level, that is, stooping to the lowest common denominator, I felt violated by this little group of well-adjusted Americans slumming the upper yard.

One of the many things that daily depresses this tale's central character, Dear Reader, is the amount of conversation around here that is devoted to laws, sentences, release dates, parole holds, and everything else to do with our shared current address. San Quentin goes on within you and without you, but always all around you.

I wrote Dave a letter yesterday. I included an envelope to my friend, Gene. I lost his address, but I sure hope he gets it. I'm quite certain that Dave will write back. He's always been the letter and postcard writer in the group.

MDC was to go through many internal changes during 1985. It would start when Franco and Dave were trying to assemble the *Peace* compilation, a very ambitious project consisting of one poet and fifty-four bands from all over the world. In addition, we would include a booklet in which each band would have a page. An awesome undertaking, and one in which Ron would have no part.

Ron had opened Fogtown Skateboards off Haight Street, and always was too busy or too this or too that to play any music. "Al was on drugs!" or "Franco's bass playing isn't good enough," or "Dave was in LA, squandering MDC's money." By the end, he had made up excuses for not playing with each of us, which he would call down from on high, hoping to gain support of another member to lend validity to another red herring, of course, only when it becomes time to work up and tune and practice, and actually do some work with those money-stealing, under-practiced, dope fiends.

Ron, at this point, couldn't relate to us. In retrospect, I think Ron had burned out on the band much as I had before they went to Europe with John. And, well, it was certain to be impossible for the crown prince of skateboards to find time in his precious schedule. They weren't asking Ron for any time to help with the compilation, just some time to work out a song so MDC wouldn't have to suffer the indignity of putting out an enormous (largest to date) compilation without an MDC song for representational purposes.

It actually worked out quite well. I had been playing with this band called Green Slime. That was a working name until a better one came along. Anyway, I get a call from Dave telling me about the comp they were doing. After snickering about the disaster all those other bands on Radical Records' singles wound up being, instead of the compilation I had proposed way back when, I told him that I was happy playing with my new band. If nothing else, I didn't need any more pain attached to my music. I told him that the thought of working with Ron again made my skin crawl. Dave said, "That works out. Ron has refused to play with us anyway."

"Okay, so, what the hell ... I'll do it!" I was also able to get Green Slime guitarist, Tom Albino, to replace the ever-industrious Mr. Ron Posner. The result was the dark and theatrical *Missile Destroyed Civilization*. I was back with Dave and MDC, then came the Gordon years.

That's "Gordon," not "golden" years, though they were good years. Gordon Frazer, our second real guitarist, was to record our next two albums (tapes, records, CDs, whatever), and do two or three trips to Europe with us, along with half a dozen excursions on this side of the Atlantic. We also got to play Hawaii. Yes, they were good years.

Gordon on guitar was followed by Eric Calhoun; that is the Eric that would have likely asphyxiated in the Vats fire had I not been there to wake him and his girl Jerry up. Ron rejoined for a tour abroad; and then Bill, the band slut; and Chris Wilder. Many different guitar spices in this musical bouillabaisse known as MDC.

19

From there to here, and back, or were we here before there? No, I distinctly remember, because the promoter in Godnosware ripped us off the night before... Remember? Huh?

I find myself again groping for the chronology of events, and feel that I've worked myself through the most painful periods of my life and times. Instead, at this point, I find it more important to write down the events, and ignore their chronological sequence. I feel that at different times I find myself more inclined to write about different things, or relate different stories.

So, to hell with tradition. I'm going to write what I'm motivated to write about, at the time I can write about it best. Boy, that's a lot off my shoulders!

I know, Dear Reader, I'm rambling again. Quentin, you know. I rot here, trying to tell of happier times, while my world outside goes to the thieves, scoundrels, and other dogs.

Dogs! Did I say dogs? I guess I'm a bit of a scoundrel myself. A literary scoundrel! Yes, folks, this is an exercise in clumsy segues, and the next segment is about my Doberman, who became infamous touring with MDC.

Touring anywhere seems to invite the presence of another animal. Yes, of course I'm referring to the pigs. You can always count on a cop being there when you don't need one. One time when we didn't need one (as if we ever did), we were driving somewhere in the Midwest. It was the middle of the night. Tammy, our road manager, was at the wheel. Glove, my Doberman, was riding or sleeping shotgun, and the rest of us are in the back of the van asleep when… Oh shit, we're being pulled over. This, of course, wakes us all up, as police lights always will. We would, of course, pretend to remain asleep in hopes that he wouldn't bother us. The cop (pig) approached the driver-side window, where he asked for the usual documentation: license, registration, and proof of insurance.

We're all good on those. He told Tammy that she was speeding, and asks her where we were headed. She replied our standard answer to that question, which was always to tell the officer (scum) that we were headed to the first major town in the next state, whatever that town happened to be. "Just passing through on our way to be someone else's problem, sir." Then the patrolman (bastard) noticed Glove lying on the passenger seat.

"Does that dog bite?" he asked.

Glove, as if on cue, picks up her head, looks the cop right in the eye, bares her teeth, and growls a low pitched but definitely menacing growl. Glove was never fond of uniforms or invasions of her territory, in this case, the van.

Tammy then meekly replied as if she were embarrassed, which she wasn't, "Well, yes," in her quaint little East Texas accent, and we were off with no ticket and a "Have a nice night, ma'am."

He neglected to say goodnight to Glove who just snorted and went back to sleep. We all laughed as we pulled away. I was never prouder of her, and we all made a fuss over MDC's cop-hating security officer. Glove wasn't always welcome unanimously. I remember Ron telling me that she wasn't any good for protection of the van, and the music equipment therein. The van wasn't safe with just her alone, and that our equipment could be "bought for a Big Mac from Glove, and if anyone had a gun, well, they would just shoot her and take our stuff."

I replied, "If anyone is pointing a gun, I personally would help them load our gear into their truck, starting with your guitar!" I think Ron realized how foolish his comments were and said nothing about it.

Bob Noxious, singer of The Fuck-ups, made Glove a spiked collar with studs that read *MDC*. She used to strut around the Vats like she owned the place with her fancy collar.

One time, while we were still living in Austin, Glove and I went to New Orleans and Baton Rouge to play a couple of shows with a band called The Sluts, whose drummer had bailed on them. The Sluts traveled in an old reconditioned hearse. That fucking hearse decides to blow a head gasket right on one of those elevated roads above the bayou. We all wind up crammed into Toxic Reasons' van all the way to Baton Rouge and back. Of course, this is the perfect timing for my young, spirited Dobey-girl to — you guessed it! — go into heat.

We completed the little tour with Glove wearing my underpants. Then, with The Sluts' hearse gone, what was I to do to get back to Austin? Did I mention that The Sluts recently had moved to Austin from... That's right, New Orleans! So, The Sluts are right at home, literally, and I... Well, I mention all of this because this story can't be told, at least not by me, without my thanking a tremendous bunch of guys who took your boy and his dog, Dear Reader, from New Orleans, Louisiana to Austin, Texas on their way to — get this — Fayetteville, Arkansas. (Consult your map.) Now that's a group of nice guys. Again, let me express Glove and my own heartfelts to Toxic Reasons for putting up with me, much less my "in season" pooch for so many miles. Miles that were way out of their way.

Years later, back home in SF, I was about to begin to relate this story to East Bay Ray of the Kennedys, when he stopped me mid-sentence. "You mean the Bloody Dog Tour?"

He said this as if it were the oldest news in town, and required reading in Punk Rock 101. I looked back at him, surprised to find out how famous my little Doberman was.

And, unlike Ron's opinion, Glove was a super watchdog. I once tested her with DRI to see if she really could be bought for a Big Mac. I was happy to find that Spike and Eric from DRI wouldn't dream of trying to break into our van after hearing the ferociousness therein.

People's Voice Benefit

MDC
from San Francisco Ca.

with The spastic rythm tarts
Dissonance,
and The crucifucks

wednesday 27 JULY
9:00 p.m.

TWO DOORS DOWN
from the Mustang Bar

1210 turner, North Lansing

20

Hold it! Stop the presses! ... for somebody was stabbed after chow in the yard. Whistles blew and buzzers sounded. We hit the ground as the COs came out of everywhere. After about an hour or so, we were strip-searched again, and of course locked down like the animals that we are. "They'll never take us alive, copper!"

Well, damn! Cops, cops, and more fucking cops. Man, what I wouldn't give just to go home for one night. Wherever that is, now that the fleecing of my belongings and the place I used to call "home" has long since had its eviction and probably has strangers living in it. Well, Dear Reader, am I having fun yet?

While cops are the present subject, I might as well mention some fellow cop-haters, The Crucifucks, with whom I was privileged to sing along with on one of the best punk rock anthems of all time, "Cops for Fertilizer," while on tour. Chorus: "Let's kill the fucking pigs if they get in our way. It'll make a good example for the children today. It'll keep 'em out of trouble, shooting pigs after school, and waste a cop will be the hero's golden rule!"

This happy youth-oriented tune was one of Doc Dart's creations, and is very fitting for one who grew up in cop-infested Flint, Michigan. Doc had put on a Flint gig, complete with posters that would be hard for Christians or police to not take umbrage at. So, in the interest of keeping an eye on the notorious pigs, he would call the cops as a "concerned citizen," posing questions like, "I'm disturbed by these posters depicting what I believe to be bands. One of them is called Millions of Dead Cops, and the other name I really can't say out loud in good conscience, and I wanted to know if you were aware of this, and if anything is being done about it."

Doc tape-records the conversations, and — what do you know? — the questions and answers, and even police threats, appear in between the cuts on their first album, along with "Cops for Fertilizer."

The police had now made it plain that it was decidedly unsafe, and even foolhardy, to hold the gig at the intended hall, so it was moved to a private residence on the outskirts of town, where we played on the garage roof. It was all way cool until some uninvited guests in blue showed up, but by then the damage was done. A parade of punks in cars followed us as we departed, escorting the van containing the band that the police knew was the Dead Cop boys, those cop-killing poster kids who find amusement in the violence that would take the life of their fellow officer. Pissed off pigs that had to stomach the fact that there was not going to be the witness-less pull-over of our van, and subsequent search and ID runs, not to mention the drugs they might find or plant. I'm sure they had a fun little time in mind for us. The escort worked perfectly, and we said our goodbyes at the end of those cops' jurisdiction.

What were those silly cops so upset about, you ask? Well, Doc's poster had pictures of policemen killed in the line of duty with Xs drawn over their eyes. Come see Millions of Dead Cops! In case that didn't do the trick, the poster also had a picture of the police academy's graduating class with the same Xs on their eyes. Coming Attractions! Those cops, tsk, tsk. No sense of humor.

Got to hand it to Doc! Another time we played on a roof was in San Francisco. Dave's apartment (AKA the "Rat House") was on Landers, right across the street from the Mission Dolores church. As fate would have it, Pope John Paul himself was going there to hold Mass. We had just put the finishing touches on the *Millions of Damn Christians* album, and thought the Pope would be delighted to have a little live sample of the first cut "This Blood's for You." As the

Pope arrived, we erupted into "This Blood" right into "Multi-Death Corporation."

About one minute later, the Secret Service and police were all over us. Again, no sense of humor. They pulled the plug on us mid-song, and escorted us to the ground. Then they carried our amps downstairs, searched the apartment, and let us go.

In the very next issue of *Maximum RocknRoll* was a picture of the police carrying our amplifiers downstairs. Underneath the picture read the caption: MDC's New Roadies. Once again, the numbskull cops unwittingly contributed to the success and notoriety of our show. We never knew whether or not the Pope enjoyed our brief performance, and no review appeared in the Vatican newspaper... or so we're told.

21

Getting back to the good old Midwest on tour, I now want to tell you about one of the most unlikely venues around.

The first time one plays The Outhouse in Lawrence, Kansas, upon your approach you're ready to kill your tour manager. At this point, for us, Mark Dubicki was that culprit.

"Where are you taking us?" we demanded. We had to be going the wrong way. We were miles from the center of town, and literally heading into a long endless corn field that would have even Stephen King thinking twice. The corn being so tall and thick that it looked like a corridor through hell.

Suddenly, a large clearing pops up out of nowhere on the right. In the middle of this clearing, which was totally invisible seconds ago, stood a single cinderblock building. Around the building was a parking area packed full of cars. Still, if you walked as little as twenty or thirty feet into the corn, you could easily not find your way back.

The Outhouse had electricity, but water had to be brought in to flush the toilets. Actually, it was perfect. A little buggy in the summer, but well known enough to be well established, and out of the way enough to allow us to do our thing without the annoyance of uninvited guests in blue. We played four times in Lawrence, always at The Outhouse, and always drew a good crowd and did well. So, if anyone ever asked, I could say unequivocally that punk rock was alive and well and living in the middle of a corn field in Kansas… "There's no place like home" sayeth both Dorothy and Ian MacKaye (*Out of Step* LP, last song,) Just click the heels of your ox-blood red Doc Marten's three times.

Lawrence, Kansas or Lincoln, Nebraska. Same diff, right? WRONG! While the cops in Lawrence left us alone, the same could not be said of their distant inbred cousins in Lincoln, unfortunately, where the hall was right downtown. We were backstage, minding our own business, watching the opening acts when — you guessed it, dear reader — some agency of the government shut down the show. I think this time it was for a fire hazard. We were all forced to leave.

Dave was in his Elvis outfit that night. He always had few off-the-wall outfits just to add some fun to the routine of touring. At one point, the Elvis suit got so mildewed and sweaty after a few shows that I renamed him "Smelvis."

Elvis or Smelvis, Dave was dressed as the King when we left the building at the gentle prodding of the police. Dave grabs his acoustic guitar, and starts singing "Love Me Tender" on the steps of our RV, the recreational vehicle that was our tour vehicle. Luckily, the captain of the police was an Elvis fan, and allowed Dave to play a few songs. Then, when the cops told us to stop, Dave went inside, and I stood outside announcing, "The King has left the auditorium."

Still, MDC, in its never-ending quest to push the envelope, took our first opportunity when the police left. Before you know it, we're around and through downtown, as if it we're our own private block party. Dave, guitar in hand, and me playing everything in sight, with a chorus of local talent a-singing "John Wayne Was a Nazi" and "Dick for Brains" at the top of our lungs. The police were not charmed by these non-Elvis-like lyrics, and were quick to start arresting people and physically dispersing others. The King was one of the first to go.

"Hey, Al! Take my guitar!" Dave called. I shoved through the me-lee and grabbed the guitar, as the police swept through the crowd and apprehended the King of Rock and Roll. Then, as I'm walking back to the van to regroup and determine where to find bail, I hear, "Hey, there he is with the guitar!"

I turned around and I'm surrounded· by five cops' clubs, a-waving at the ready to break my head in. It wasn't long before I was joining Dave in the Lincoln hoosegow. We got bailed out, and they eventually sent Dave some papers closing the case, and clearing his good name. I, however, being more transient at that time, never got any papers.

So, I may still be a wanted man in Nebraska. As a result, whenever we're in Nebraska, I'm plagued by my band telling me to "Get in the van," or else "Stay backstage or out of sight."

While I may be a wanted man in Nebraska, Dave is a criminal mastermind and drug lord when we get to the Canadian border.

We were traveling from Rock Island, Iowa to Winnipeg, Alberta, Canada. This is about an eighteen-hour drive. We get to the Canadian border at Blackpool, North Dakota. Now, a bit of history is called for: Ten years before, in Austin, Texas, Dave had a flourishing little pot business. One day, some transient that Dave had allowed to stay over, from of the kindness of his heart, snitched him out. When the cops broke in, he had a garbage bag full of Mexi-sense. Fortunately, he had planned for such a contingency, and when it occurred, he was able to hire the best defense money could buy. The fellow's name was Philip Pressy. A good lawyer, at least in Texas, is a lawyer who is a friend of the judge. A couple of regular good ole boys, in fact. In court, it went like a charm. Dave's case was called early.

"Hello, Judge," began Mr. Pressy.

"Hello there, Phil," replied the judge. "How are Sarah and the kids?"

"Just fine," Dave's attorney replied. "And your family?"

"All well, thanks," said the judge. "And what do you have today?"

"Well, Judge, we got this nice college boy, and he's got himself into a bit of trouble. He's real sorry though, and I believe him when he says he'll never do it again. We were sure hoping that you might see fit to give him a break, this being his first offense and all."

And sure as the sky is blue, that twenty pounds became an under-an-ounce, simple possession, judge-dismissed, with a stern warning. Got to love that legal system! However…

Ten years later, here we are, MDC at the Canadian border, getting sweated by immigration and customs cops. First, they have me in the little office, and they're asking all sorts of questions about my criminal past. I told them that I had never been arrested. The big fat senior pig was not pleased with that little declaration. I'm not sure if he really didn't believe me, or if it was because no arrests meant he would have no reason to fuck with me. At any rate, all he had to say was, "You had better be telling the truth, because if we find out you're lying then you'll really be in trouble," and some other *blah blah, woof woof.*

Truthfully, I was kind of nervous because, well, I was lying, and, in fact, had been arrested numerous times. Then he said something about a DUI that I had supposedly forgotten to mention. I knew he was just fishing, and I was home free. I never had a DUI!

Next was Dave, to endure the same scrutiny. All of a sudden… Could I have heard right?… Did I actually hear right????… AM I REALLY HEARING THIS??!!??? Is this some FUCKING NIGHT-MARE?!

No, I am hearing Dave, complete with big brown, honest, sincere eyes relating the ten-year-old tale of the long-forgotten possession incident in Texas. I see the border guard smirk at me.

At this point I just up put my feet on the chair next to me, put on my sunglasses, folded my arms in a contemptuous fashion, and grinned a "fuck you, pig" kind of sneer back at him.

The senior pig says that Dave can't go in without some ministry papers that would takes days, if not weeks, to secure. When I said that no, I didn't want to go without him, nor did I have any business that I could do there without Dave, he wrote something down on my application and thanked me.

Now, I've crossed too many borders not to know better, and I asked for my application back. The guard told me that once a form was filed, he was not empowered to rescind it. "Well then," I said, "I guess I'll just have to cross the border and come right back." The guard begrudgingly returned the form. He handed my application back, and, boy, I was right. The words appeared prominently, "Entry refused," as was written on Dave's application as well.

"You're pretty smart, wise guy," the guard said.

"Well, ONE of us has to be!" I replied looking over at my verbose friend. That guard was right, for if I had left with that Refused Entry on the border computer, it would have popped up every time I wished to get into Canada, and maybe into anywhere out of the USA.

To the horror of the Winnipeg promoter, Mike Lambert, who was financially extended to the eyeballs, we turned and left Canada. You could tell that the fat, bald guard's day was made as he merrily informed us that if we tried to return through another border crossing or another shift, we would arrested for... I don't recall what the charge was, but I believed him.

Mike Lambert has been a friend and ally for many years, and the closing down of these two shows in Winnipeg not only cost us dearly — namely $1500 in guarantees just in Winnipeg alone, plus merchandise (records, tapes, and t-shirts) sales — but poor Mike. He took it on the chin, and kept on — well, maybe not smiling — but kept on, never the less. Mike had laid out for a hall for two nights, including whatever the Canadian version of insurance and security was, advertising, and a bunch for t-shirts. Sure, he'd eventually recover from the t-shirts, but without a show to sell them at, that cash would be tied up for months.

Now, for MDC, it hurt, but we'd recover. After all, there was always another day with another show in another town, hopefully with another decent guarantee. The promoter has no such relief, especially in a far-off place like Winnipeg.

Promotion in punk is another one of those two-sided coins of which I have spoken. This sort of disaster is the kind of thing that the punk rockers don't mention when they talk mindlessly about "greedy promoters," claiming that they are all rich and exploiting punk rock. These naysayers have neither the ability nor the will to stick out their lazy necks for punk or anything else. However, the same opinionated big mouths seem to have all kinds of time and ability to talk badly of those they see as doers, as opposed to talkers. So I'm glad to have an opportunity to thank Mike and many others who share his thankless and risky profession, that being promoting and putting on shows of bands that they believe in. (Anti-sellouts, if you ask me.) Especially in a town as far off the beaten path as Winnipeg, where, at least back then, hardly any bands ever went, someone like Mike, and those like him, DO make the event at which the others have something to support. So at the risk of being repetitious… Thank you, Mike, you're a hell of a nice guy and a major bro.

Now, I had to relate the story of Dave's little pot business to explain why we were refused entry into Canada. I had to explain this refusal to set up the frame of mind we found ourselves in upon our return from almost going to Canada.

Things sometimes happen for a reason. Well, I don't believe in predestination so I really don't expect you, Dear Reader, to believe it either. I do think you make your luck sometimes, even if you can't tell where you might end up at the time. Following your convictions will hopefully get you where you can stand to be, if not where you want to be.

At any rate, you can make the most of almost any situation. Fucking hell, look where I'm writing this from. Better yet, don't look. I'm absolutely certain that I never would have had the… "time" was the word I was going to say, but truthfully, it's discipline that I wouldn't find to accomplish such a lengthy task. Hell, I couldn't even get my homework done when I was in school. I'm quite sure that I wasn't thinking, "I'd better not get passing grades, or else I won't have go to the University of Tampa, where I am destined to meet the singer of my band and lifelong comrade with whom I will tour the world." No, I was not exactly lazy, more preoccupied with anything and everything if it had nothing to do with school. It's dumb luck… I didn't set myself up to meet Dave. So, I do believe in Murphy and his law.

So, here's the thing: We're driving back from the Canadian border. Mark Dubicki, our road manager, is driving, I'm riding shotgun, and it's the middle of the night. We are outside a small town in North Dakota called Pembina. We are all feeling low having just been denied what would surely have been packed gigs. Everyone else is asleep in the back. I'm staring mindlessly at the horizon when... What the hell is that? It looks like a gigantic blow torch right on the edge of the horizon. But this thing would have had to be hundreds of feet tall! I looked over to Mark and asked him what he thought we might be looking at when I noticed the same thing on the opposite horizon. Mark was as baffled as me. I told him to pull over. I needed to stretch my legs anyway. I get out and look up.

"Hey, Mark, check this shit out!" I am looking up at these streams of light extending from the blow torches all the way up to the center of the sky. Where they met, there were these little colorful strips of I-don't-know-what that kept pulsing and changing color. Bright colors, like green and purple. Then, I heard the crackling. An electrical kind of noise amid the dancing stripes. All this was so far up that it had to be enormous! The spectacle did some little fluctuation and color change, and I just whooped! By this time, the crew was awake. I said for everyone to get out here and see this... this. I still had no clue. We were all whooping and hollering moments later. Unbelievable!

Well, we spent the next hour and a half staring at the show, a laser light show the full length and breadth of the sky.

The next day we were to read about "The Most Dramatic Display of the Northern Lights in Recent History!" The article sort of explained it as a freak occurrence that involved a buildup of electricity and ice high in the atmosphere, combined with Northern Lights, and high and low atmospheric pressure, and some other speculative scientific jargon, that may or may not have been the truth. But, in fact, no one we spoke to in town could remember anything like it, and we were there. Had we been playing in Winnipeg at the time, we would have missed it.

At the time, we probably would have forgone the indulgence of the Lights to save our financial asses, but I, for one, think as it falls into perspective, it was worth it.

On our next tour, we went to see the Grand Canyon. I commented to Dave that compared to the Lights of North Dakota, the Grand

Canyon wasn't nearly as grand, it was just a fancy hole in the ground. Yeah, now, if you took the Grand Canyon and held the Northern Lights above it, then you'd really have something! (Some people are never satisfied.)

22

While I'm relating these stories about borders and Dave's way of making aces out of eights or talking his way into being denied entry, it reminds me of another time where it seemed that all was lost in Malmo, Sweden.

After the usual getting tossed by the customs people, we thought we were out of the woods. Just wait for our passports to come back from immigration, and we'll be on our way to shows in Gavle and Stockholm. Gee whiz, it seems to be taking a long time, doesn't it? I suspected that it might have something to do with the other band, who shared the next few shows, trying to cross with us.

Oh, coincidence after coincidence, and whaddya know?! Somehow one number is missing from our work visas. Yes, I felt that the guards got a good look at Stephen, the lead singer of the False Prophets, and Holy Harry Houdini, Batman! Numbers off secured documents aren't matching up in their computer.

Stephen is an original: he wears a long leather, spiky hair, and I think his most endearing feature is his nails. One hand, in particular, has outrageously long fingernails. This hand has one nail in particular, I think it's the pinky, but this thing is about nine inches long. Say, good name for a band, huh? This manicurist's worst nightmare is so fragile that he had it wrapped in black electrical tape. Completing Stephen's "ensemble" is a lovely walking stick shalalee, with an adorable real monkey's head as its handle.

So now the border guards have us sitting in our vehicles, having refused to allow us to bring our merchandise in, telling us that there is "no way" that the officers present have the authority to override this computer glitch involving one missing number on our working permits. "Sorry, no way," etc.

Well, Dave gets tired of waiting, grabs his acoustic guitar, and walks to the guards' office.

"Where do you think you're going?" we asked.

Before an answer could come, Dave was gone. Fifteen minutes later, Dave rushes back. I'm thinking, "What now?... we're under arrest... call the Consulate... they're going to march us to the wall, last cigarette anyone?"

To my amazement, Dave says, "Hurry up, let's get going!" I'm thinking Dave's lost his mind. He wants to run for it. But no! Dave had sat there, looking sad, playing "Folsom Prison Blues," and I'll be damned if the head honcho guard wasn't a Johnny Cash fan. He told Dave, "Alright, I'm turning my head, reading my book. Now, you guys get out of here and I never saw you."

We couldn't believe it. My unsinkable Dave had done it again! He had charmed the Swedish gestapo at Malmo, and before you could say, "I hear that train a-comin'...," we were a-going.

So, to recap what we have learned here, Dear Reader, with Dave at borders, you win a few, you lose a few. I guess that's how it is in punk rock — in general — as I can tell you from my present surroundings, namely, San Quentin. I guess life itself is a crapshoot of the same order.

For example, there was one time that MDC tried to get into England to play with Crass. The Crass anarchist way of dealing with (or should I say not dealing with?) government agencies for things like working papers doesn't always go over well with the border officials. We were already in their computer, anyway. When our individual names were punched in, they came out to tell us that, and I quote: "You and your 'Thousands of Dead Policemen' band are unwelcome."

We were very fortunate that our Amsterdam promoter was on the ball, so our deportation wasn't back to the USA. England was happy to be rid of us, and if Holland would have us, they deserved whatever they got. What they got was a very grateful group, pleased to the marrow just to still be in Europe. And if one has to be without shows in England, what better place to lick one's wounds than in the hash bars of Holland, I mean, "coffee houses."

Now, to break up the bordering on boredom, that is to say the monotony of borders and the crossing of same, allow me one final chance to hopefully be entertaining.

Far and away, the most unique border crossing we ever successfully attempted was crossing into Canada for, appropriately enough, and hypothetically, of course, the Anarchist Convention in Toronto. Again, the good old anarchist method. This time, however, it was our choice. Well, maybe not totally our choice as, due to our shady past transgressions, we would certainly meet with conflict at the border. Why, it's those old enemies of the Commonwealth, that seditious organization, that MDC! This was especially true, due to the well-advertised (and not necessarily all positive) nature of an event such as this gathering of those who would live by no structured rules and laws. Yes, I believe that the Ontario government would have let us sit this one out, if they could.

This time, the Toronto Anarchists — aware of our support record with Native Americans, especially those in Big Mountain and Mercury, Nevada — called upon the nearby Akwesasne tribe to help. This tribe was perhaps the most political Native American group, being the publisher of the only political magazine of the American Indian movement.

These people really helped us. After showing us their publishing operation and command center — very impressive, I might add — they took us onto tribal land, where we crossed the Saint Lawrence Seaway into Canada in a small outboard motorboat. When we reached the other side, we were hurried off and told to hide in the woods until the Anarchists could come pick us up. The Indians hurried away, further confirming our suspicions that this was a very risky business. Soon, Dan Smith and Andy Sunfrog were whisking us off to

TO in somebody's fairly new Hyundai.

I guess this is what is truly meant by "karma." MDC had done benefits for the Native Americans that the government was trying to force off their land, to get to the uranium underneath. We did raised eleven hundred dollars in one LA gig for the legal funds to help stop this treachery. Not only did we give them support, but we actually went and played for and met with the elders at Big Mountain. I don't know if they really appreciated the music, but it was obvious that our help was appreciated. Now, years later, on the other side of the continent, the name "MDC" still meant enough to another tribe to move them to stick out their necks for us. Hypothetically, of course. Thanks.

Our next rabbit to be pulled out of our proverbial hats was how to play at a well-advertised show, with your name splattered all over the posters, and sneak it by the already pissed off TO police. The fittingly named "Apocalyse" on Queen Street was to be the arena of this bit of prestidigitation.

"Ladies and Gentleman! For your entertainment pleasure, at great expense, not one but FOUR executions all at once. Hell, even Governor Wilson couldn't pull that one off!"

Well, MDC weren't going to allow this to occur, so in a moment of brilliance, I hatched a plan. I noticed that Scream's new album sported prominent pictures of the band. Unquestionable identification of who Scream was, or more importantly, who they weren't!

With the help of the band Scream from DC, whom we had known for years, a bit of changing the batting order was just what the doctor ordered. Scream, including Dave Grohl, who later went on to drum for Nirvana and play guitar and sing for the Foo Fighters (shameless name-dropping, if you ask me) agreed to play in our slot. We even made up a backstage "on stage" list to indicate that they were indeed supposed to play after MDC, just to cover their asses should there be any trouble.

So, on we went, with Dave announcing that we were Scream out of Washington, DC, after which we immediately broke into "Dead Cops" with a little fudging on the lyrics. "Red crops, wet mops, chin ups," and whatever came into Dave's mind. We finished, and wasted no time in leaving the stage and the hall.

Sure as you're born, when Scream hit the stage, they were accompanied by police, lots of police. By that time, we were gone, daddy, gone. Scream, fortunately, had albums with photos that proved that they were not MDC, not the seditious scourge that the cops were so interested in. Damn that sneaky, slippery MDC! Ha!

The next day, we were supposed to play outside for the Anarchists, but after all the other bands had been approached in their vans by the cops and asked if they were MDC, well, we opted to send our favorite country singer to fill in. That country crooner was none other than Lonesome Dave, or as he was also known, Boxcar Dave, America's favorite homo.

Just another one of the many sides to a complicated guy. Yup, Dave does have more faces than Lon Chaney. Well, amazingly, everyone knew what was going on, except for the numbskulls in blue, and a complete set of MDC's songs was performed, even if only one member did the performing. Another case of MDC pulling the wool over the policemen's eyes. Another thoroughly enjoyable afternoon was had by all.

We later returned to the States in separate vehicles so as not to be discovered as MDC. To avoid being asked for ID at the border, the infamous Texas pot dealer, Dave, took the Greyhound to Buffalo... just an American tourist coming home from a quick jaunt to Canada. It was truly Anarchy in the USA and Canada.

Back to the unpleasant reality du jour... (Where does he get this *du jour* stuff?!) Actually, in case your French is a bit stale, *du jour* means "of the day" as in "Soup du jour." (... French lessons, Christ, what next?!) So, by "reality du jour," I'm referring to my reality of the day, meaning Lockdown in Quentin.

I finally got a chance to talk to my kids for the first time in six weeks. It's the longest period of time I've ever gone incommunicado from my family. I've been gone longer, but never without calling at least once a week. Happily, the kids are in good spirits, and I'd left enough money from my "drug lord" career to see them through handsomely. Yes, I earned quite a bit dealing speed. As respectable a dealer as one could be, I'd like to think.

I was just another businessman dealing in commodities, paying his taxes with H&R West Block. (A sense of humor is essential in here.)

23

My celly and I got to talking about booking and inevitably MDC's favorite little device came up. After killing countless hours on the phone and, as a result, killing all of our good names as far as the phone company was concerned, a fellow from Canada introduced us to what we came to call "ocean in bottle" (spoken in a Russian sounding accent).

The nickname came from a movie called *The Russians are Coming, The Russians are Coming*. In the movie, the Russians, led by Alan Arkin, go into a town near Martha's Vineyard (I think) having come ashore because their malfunctioning guidance equipment had left them completely off course and lost.

They wander into a souvenir shop and find one of those clear plastic cylinders full of some thick blue oil and some clear fluid that won't mix together. When you turn the tube slowly it causes an effect that looks like waves in the ocean. It's called an "Ocean in a Bottle." They all stand gazing in amazement, and in unison say, "Ocean in bottle."

Well, we were equally amazed when a guy from Canada showed us this modified telephone dialer. With a Radio Shack phone dialer, and a chip imported from Canada, a soldering iron, and a little know-how, we were shown how to create the marvel that mimics the sound of coins being dropped into a pay telephone.

Hey, it works great for Europe, too. We eventually abbreviated it to just "Ocean." Hypothetically (your honor) MDC could have, that is, of course, if MDC were anything but people of the highest scruples, saved tens of thousands of dollars with our little Ocean. A better estimation would be to say fifty thousand, though even that's conservative... hypothetically speaking, of course.

The rewired and re-chipped "Ocean" had only four buttons that were of any importance. The other buttons just served to disguise the Ocean as a typical phone dialer. One button was the on/off switch. The other buttons that mattered were the five cent, ten cent, and the very popular twenty-five cent button. Ah, yes, the good old twenty-five cent-er with its beautiful *Beep——beep-beep——beep-beep* sound. Four presses on that button equals one dollar! What could be easier? The beautiful thing was that until the coin box is opened, there was no way for them to even notice any discrepancy. That, and the fact that there is no way for them to figure out who or where or when made the free calls.

Brilliant, huh? Occasionally, the pay phone would call back asking for twenty-five or fifty cents for overtime. We'd press the appropriate button on our little Ocean, and presto! the reply would come, "Thank you for using ATT!" That phrase always made jokes and the like, MDC, in all its wisdom has created names for certain different things. For example, as one travels through Europe the languages constantly change. Some people who will insist that they only speak one language and English, in fact speak a dialect we in MDC call "Euro." To be able to speak "Euro" basically means that from Trondeheim, Norway to Valencia, Spain, to Pulo, Croatia, they can get you to the gig on time. Sometimes "Euro" is a combination of so many different dialects that it sounds like no human language. (That's a Polish expression.)

Another thing that constantly changes is the money. (Nowadays, there's only one currency for most of Europe: the Euro, but it was different back when this was written, and it's obvious why they needed to make the change.) Overnight, one can drive from the land of lira (Italy), through the lands of Swiss francs to Austrian schillings to German marks (Germany), and wake up at a coffeehouse in Holland spending Dutch guilders.

Well, before the currency du jour situation becomes clear, especially when our heads are foggy we call them "Klondikes." So, you might have heard one of us ask another if he has any klondikes and how many of them are there to a dollar. I'm not sure where or when or who started calling them that, but it works. When, however, we started traveling in Eastern Europe and western Asia, where the value of money fluctuates daily and the average denomination is, well, a polish ziolti is, at our last time there, worth a thirteen hundred and fiftieth of a dollar. That is to say that there were one thousand, three hundred and fifty Polish zioltis to one dollar. One ziolti is worth practically nothing. You need three hundred zioltis to buy a book of matches.

At any rate, due to the sharp differences in parity and stability, and the fact that Eastern currency is not exchangeable and therefore worthless outside of the country of origin, I nicknamed this sort of money, also called "soft" currency, "Kreploches." It somehow seemed to fit.

So, in recapping, Dear Reader, when traveling through Europe with MDC, pounds, francs (French or Swiss or Belgian), lira, marks, markas, pesadas, crowns, kroners, guilders, schillings and of course, dollars are Klondikes. Rubles, zioltis, denars, and the like are Kreploches.

It's very hard to exchange kreploches for klondikes as I've said, and even in the country that issues them, hard currency is greatly preferred. If one wished to rent a PA (public address) system in Moscow, one would need klondikes, not rubles.

I once tried to buy some matroishka dolls in St. Petersburg, formerly Leningrad, Russia. The woman heard my American accent and lit up like a Christmas tree. "How much?" I asked, indicating a particular doll that I thought my daughter, Marie, might like. "Seven dollars," she replied.

"No, in rubles," I said. She glared, and said to me, "What have I done so an American should come all the way here to pay me in rubles? No dollars?" she asked. I felt badly and kind of awkward but we struck a bargain that I'm sure was to her advantage. That was all right with me, too. After all, we had to spend all our rubles before we left the country anyway. Rubles, back in '92 couldn't be exchanged for other currencies.

We bought dolls and trinkets, MOCKBA (Moscow) watches, lighters, and all sorts of other stuff, but the best thing that Chris and I brought back from Russia were chess sets. Mine was red and black, which I far preferred to black and white.

"They say the darkest hour is just before the dawn. In chess, without exception, white moves the first pawn." Those are the first words of the title cut of our record *Shades of Brown*. My chess set was the exception though. Red made the first move on my board.

Back in the Big Q, where phone calls are practically impossible except for the block workers and tier tenders, this fellow Dan, a block worker, made a phone call for me. I asked him to call MDC's bass player, Erica. She was the last of five bass players we had to date. I had her telephone number memorized, but I didn't have an address for her. I really wanted to write to her.

We had met while I was playing for this other band, Gecko Valour. She auditioned, and got the bass-playing job although her chops needed work. At that time, Gecko Valour consisted of three women and three men, including Erica and me. Funny how you can get the wrong impression of someone. I guess I was just paranoid, but I got the impression that she didn't care for me. Granted, I was a bit of a tweeker, and that doesn't always go over with everyone. I think that she thought the same thing, I mean, that I didn't like her. So for a few rehearsals we kind of ignored each other.

I've always been a kind of leader of rehearsals, not the only one or someone who was sensitive to everyone's needs and ideas. I think that knowing what it takes to make progress, and also understanding that the best kind of band is one that shares its ideas and therefore belongs to all the members, makes for a good leader. More or less it's keeping the focus and pace. This, however, can intimidate a newcomer. I think this was part of my sketchy start with Erica. It was amplified, I think, by the fact that we really did want to have the approval of the other.

It wasn't long, though, until I could unequivocally say that she was my favorite bass player of all that I had ever had the pleasure of working and playing with. So let me complete my thought on what won her my approval. She wasn't bad at first, but being the drummer, and therefore closely aligned with the bass line, I couldn't help but notice where her weaknesses were.

At our second rehearsal, I was full on ready to hear her struggle through the same parts that had given her problems at the first rehearsal... Well, much to my surprise, the parts that had been weak were now extra tight! Her progress continued at a very capable rate, so that when MDC was looking for a bass player — Matt had just quit to go and start a new band with his old guitarist Tim... that little band is now Rancid — I was discussing our bass-less plight with Dave over the telephone after a Gecko rehearsal at Gecko's rehearsal spot, namely the Diesel Cathedral on South Van Ness, and Erica overheard me talking. I had given her a *Millions of Damn Christians* tape just to listen to, and she caught me quite by surprise when she said, in that endearing but not presumptuous style, "I'd like to try, I think I could do it."

I'd learned many things from my experience with Gecko. One was how natural it felt to play with women in the band, and another was that if you really liked who you were playing with then it's easier to put in all the time you need to get where you're going musically. MDC, with all its side and interwoven business interests, had allowed me to forget why I was a musician in the first place. It all came back to me then. I knew that second that Erica was going to be our next (and hopefully last) bass player even if it took forever, because I had nothing better to do than work with people I really wanted to be working with.

A band being so many things to so many people, a musical marriage of multiple members, and if the music isn't feeling good then all the rest goes quickly from labor of love to a burden of misrepresentation and heartache. I'd seen that happen to me and Dave too many times before. Michelle Shocked, the folksinger, is credited with the saying: "Music is far too important to be left to professionals." MDC had some of the most talented people to be found anywhere among its alumni, yet keeping a solid band together year in and year out seemed to be an illusive proposition, at best. (More philosophy, Mr. PhD? Funny, I don't remember signing up for Long-windedness 101.)

Okay, okay, Dear Reader, there's no reason to get nasty. Anyway, the news of the phone call to Erica that my fellow convict, Dan, made for me was that she not only gave me her address, but Holy cow! She wanted a visiting form!

She was planning to come see me as soon as she got approved. Hot damn! Of course, this excitement would soon wear out to a more melancholy feeling of just how much I miss her and everyone else, and how much I miss making music with her. I wonder if we are even going to play together again. Sigh.

Michelle Shocked, by the way, lived up to her saying one tour, when the "hot shit" hired guns that the label had to support became a bit insubordinate. So she fired them and finished the tour solo. Right on, Michelle! Oh, that ability to go on solo. I do envy her that.

24

MDC, or at least the part of it that calls himself "Al," has always appreciated the privilege of being able to almost survive, doing what we like to do, as much as we love traveling and making music. Some places we played multiple times, and while playing for new people in new places is always an adventure, going back to some others is like visiting and revisiting an old friend. One of these very special places is the Leon Cavalo in Milan (Milano), Italy.

I recall the first time we played there. Upon entering I couldn't help but notice the cornerstone saying 1392. Man, one hundred years before what's-his-name came from Europe to "bring civilization" to the red-skinned "heathens."

The Leon Cavalo is a huge squat with a half a dozen buildings, or more. In the main building is a tremendous hall and gathering place. That's where the shows were put on. We played there a total of four times. One of my very favorite shows — maybe my favorite show ever — occurred on our third time there.

We were in a weird mood. Dave, countering the Italian version of machismo, was wearing a dress, and was stunning, I must say. We all decided to start the show with "Politician." Now, a bit of history is needed to understand the political significance of this hall.

The Leon Cavalo is historically famous for being the political gathering place for the poorer Italians. It offered asylum at difficult times to some of the persecuted groups throughout Italy's lengthy history. In recent years, the police had tried to shut it down numerous times by force of one sort or another. This time the cops had blown away a whole corner of the hall. I was never sure how. Scaffolding and blue plastic covered the hole, which had to measure fifty feet across and thirty feet high.

Those Italian squatters are unstoppable, however. It was winter and a bit cold, but the show must go on. So, we thought, although we had never started with a slow number before, tonight, for the first time, at this huge, thousand-plus people show at the famous Leon Cavalo, we were going to start with "Politician."

We get to the first "Hey there, baby," and the entire place loses power. The lights, the amps, the PA, everything! All of a sudden, the crowd starts cheering and lighting lighters and matches. Then, as the matches turned to torches, and the crowd got wilder, yours truly knows what must be done.

Well, you can kill the amplifiers by shutting the power, and the vocals by shutting down the PA system, but the drums? Well, that's quite another matter. Even without the benefit of amplification in a huge stone room, drums are vibrant, though reverby, and as a result, loud. I seized the energy of the moment. I was on top of my game, and played an extremely rare drum solo. I was all charged up for a whole show, and had all the energy in the world. So, for what seemed like two minutes but was really ten or fifteen, I soloed my heart out amid the cheers of the crazed, appreciative, and demonstrative Italians.

When the power and lights returned, I was bushed but I could never be too tired to play for people like that. Italy has always been good to MDC... I think that they remember back to 1984.

The first time we came to Italy, we played for a country suffering the worst recession since the War (WWII). We knew that they knew that we knew, back then, that MDC was going to do nothing but lose money playing for the money the punk rockers in Italy could afford... They knew we just wanted to play for them, and the money wasn't what we were there for.

Most other bands wouldn't come down to Italy for that reason. It was easier and more economical to play in Germany and Holland.

Even England had more money to spread around than poor, down-trodden Italy in 1984. Now, with the economy in a better state, we still play for far less than many bands, after all, we are still playing mostly for punk rockers and squatters and the like. Our draw is very strong in Italy, though, and when in Italy, we do make out and make out well If you were to ask any of us about Italy, we would be likely to reply "Molto bene."

By our next trip to the Leon Cavalo, the missing wall had been re-built. Although the cinderblocks didn't have the charm of the original wall, and the 1392 cornerstone was lost forever, the new wall some-how made a statement by just being there, and strong. When I saw it I had to smile. Long live the Leon Cavalo and the irrepressible spirit of the people that keep it alive.

Another incredible venue is a fort in Rome or a "Forte" in Roma. The Forte Prenestino sits atop one of the seven hills of Rome. It was built there to protect Rome from invaders during the twelfth century. It's a creepy little castle-like structure, with double walls surrounding the inner building, passages and tunnels run throughout. The World Series of Hide and Go Seek couldn't take place in a better place.

We slept over there one night after a show. We were literally scared to tell ghost stories so as not to disturb the residents of past eras that certainly would inhabit such a place. It wasn't long before I was to try and test this moratorium. I began, "Well, there is a legend about a very unpleasant event," using a rather haunting voice. Abruptly, almost in unison, it was strongly suggested that I might "Shut the fuck up!" The Forte's so grown in the ground that it does put one in mind of a huge gravestone in a cemetery on a hill.

The stage was erected on a scaffold in the middle of a long, thin courtyard created by the inner and outer walls. In the open air, be-neath the stars, and in Rome, to boot: you can't get more romantic than that. MDC's shows at the Forte were always attended by thou-sands, and even at three or four thousand lira apiece (eleven hundred lira to the dollar), we always made out. In fact, in Italy, at eleven hun-dred to a buck, we made millions!

Dave had been careless a week before we left on tour once, and had left my drums in the van in the Mission, SF, and guess what? David Copperfield must have been in town, because to our amazement, the drums disappeared! Well, my friend and attorney Chip came to our rescue... One of the many life saving deeds brother Chip would make for me and mine. He loaned us the money to replace the kit, and told me since we could make payments on his credit card, not to chump myself, and to get a smoking drumset. I bought a beautiful set of Pearl BLX birchwood, with the wood grain actually visible through a rich blue stain.

I brought them over to Europe and down to Rome. Can't get more romantic than that! We were so rushed timewise that I had to send them over unassembled, still in the crates. I first put them together — set the heads, rims, and lugs, mounts and legs — on the stage at the Forte.

Have I mentioned how I love Italian audiences? Their emotional, demonstrative, passionate appreciation is like no other. Not to slight anyone else, but if I had to play my last show before I died and could pick the venue, it would probably be The Forte or the Leon Cavalo, but probably The Forte just for the allure of being in Rome. That way when I completed the last drum riff of my career, I could smile, and say, "Arrivederci, Roma!" Just breaks your heart, don't it, Dear Reader? (Reader wipes eyes free of crocodile tears.)

Another town I love is Berlin. We've played a half a dozen or so places there, but I think my favorite is a club called The X. It's an L-shaped hall, and really packs up when a band is playing, since the part of the crowd in the "panhandle" of the L squeezes toward the center in order to see.

It was there we met Jenny, the Rat Woman. This nickname was earned through her passion for rats. Pet rats, that is. She always had one or more in her pocket, or up her sleeve. One time, we were leaving Berlin and Jenny was with us. We stopped at one of the Intrashoppes. This was on our first tour, before the fall of the Berlin Wall, and we were naive and nervous. Communist countries have an unsettling energy about them. They have it set up that way to keep pressure on their population. I've mentioned already what these Intrashoppes were like.

It was Christmas time 1982, and our first time in a communist country. Somehow, as if in a movie, graceful old Dave manages to get his coattail caught on the shop's Christmas tree. TIMBER! The whole damn tree comes tumbling down. Remember in the flick *Animal House*, when they shoot the horse with blanks that gives him a heart attack, and run down the hall yelling, "Holy shit!" You get the idea.

We dash out of the store, jump in the car, and before we could even get out of the end of the parking lot... "Pull it over!" We pull it over, and starting singing and whistling the theme from the TV show *Hogan's Heroes* with Dave telling us how he didn't think it was funny. I thought, he's right, it's not funny. Rather clumsy, but certainly not funny. I didn't have the nerve to tell him that just then.

Soon the descendants of Coronal Klink were again yelling that nasty sounding German at us. But this time, although we didn't know it, we were prepared. Our secret weapon, Jenny, starts shouting and growling right back at them. I don't know what she said but it wiped the smug right off their faces. Before you could say "Jenny Uber Alles" We were off again ... Man, be careful if you ever find yourself wanting to marry a German National, Dear Reader.

In MDC, we had an expression, whose origin I never knew: "Life's too short to learn German," but sometimes we've been glad that some people have bothered.

Berlin is also where we recorded our live album *Elvis Does the Rhineland* at the Quarter Latin. Yes, the Latin quarter of West Berlin in East Germany. You figure it out. There's never been a Latin sector with a Checkpoint Chico, to my knowledge. At any rate, it's a beautiful theater. We played there with Ludichrist. What a wild bunch, those guys. The live record is an import on Destiny Records.

Now, here's another town that I could do without: San Quentin, California. It's a sunny Saturday here except for in my dark little cell. My neighbor's a man named Glen P. Glen prides himself on being a convict. Should you call him an inmate, he will tell you emphatically that he is a Convict. He loves to give the guards a hard time. He's just doing his job as a convict. Glen has my full respect. He reminds me a lot of Alphonso S. at San Bruno. He runs his own little store from his cell and is the main link-up on the "wire" or "phone." The phone is just yelling around from one cell to another, like, "Hey, one-fifteen, you got those cigarettes for four-sixty-three?"

"Yeah!"

"Hey, four sixty-three, you got those envelopes for one-fifteen?"

"Yeah…" and so the transaction is completed, through tier runners and block workers and, occasionally, by fishing. However, no word would have gotten through without the robust voice of Mr. Peoples in three-eighteen.

Glen, as he's permitted me to call him, has never played that black/white thing that I've seen. Most of the people here have to. It's a way of life around here. I'm glad some people don't need to. Glen and I have achieved OG status, OG standing for Original Gangster or Old Guy. That buys one a little play in avoiding having to "Tip Up" with one gang or another. Youngsters have a lot more pressure to join. Still OG status or not, one doesn't go anywhere alone or jump in anyone's "mix," lest one find oneself in a "wreck."

Consequences of such an altercation can be dire indeed. Many have "slipped" to their deaths off a tier or were stabbed in the yard. Vigilance and respect are the watchwords in here. I was trying to give Redman some butter off my plate this morning. I accidentally dropped some on my celly's sleeve. He looked at me so hard that I just had to laugh although I know the serious nature of what I had done. Had my celly and I not been good friends, this accident could be misconstrued. Before you know it, you have a fight on your hands.

You might want to consider that many, if not most, of the people you might encounter here are no strangers to violence. No one got here by being too nice or gentle. Even a little fistfight can be deadly. The gunners are always ready to shoot first and ask questions later. Nobody guarantees your safety here, and nobody has ever won a wrongful death suit against the California Department of Corrections. Talk about your wrong place at the wrong time! Reader, this the wrong place anytime.

I can see a slice of San Francisco Bay outside my cell across the tier through a distant window. In the Bay, I can occasionally see a boat or two, with people enjoying the Memorial Day weekend… a Memorial Day I will have lost forever.

I have started to equate my term here with a voyage on an ocean-going vessel: a slow, slow boat to and from Hell.

Well, I'm halfway through my sentence now. It's as if I've reached my destination, and I'm turning around and heading home. I'm not sure where that will be. I suppose that there are few places that I wouldn't prefer to my present address… that is, San Quentin State Prison.

Quentin, as we inmates — I mean, convicts — refer to her, lends new meaning to another MDC expression gleaned from our old road manager's father. And I quote: "It's a long day… but a short life." The day in Quentin is indeed long, and without the aforementioned vigilance, a short life is a distinct possibility.

25

Throughout my travels, and all its high times and thrills, I have to thank someone with whom we never traveled. She never left home, and still gave me the biggest kick in over seventy-five cities from Honolulu to Moscow. (Riddles, it's come to this? Okay, I give up. Why did the chicken cross the road?) No, Dear Silly Reader, it's "Why did the policeman cross the road?" The answer is, "To go and hassle the chicken!"

Now, as I was saying, this person was responsible for so many great times that I can't thank her enough. She is China, and although we never were married, we comprised a concerned, caring, parenting team. China, after much soul-searching and consideration, allowed me to take her little bundle of joy, our son Brian, on tour with MDC. For this privilege, I will be forever in her debt. I don't weigh lightly the faith she placed in me allowing me to take a four-year-old around America, and later to Europe when he turned six. I turn now to some of my happiest recollections. Travels, times, and places I was able to share with my son.

It's most ironic that Brian should see his father on the other side of the spectrum, in jail. He's seen the deference people have shown to me while on tour, and even sycophantic throngs in exotic places. He knows his hot drumming, big shot daddy as a member of MDC, and now he's seen his dad in county jail orange. I don't think I could bear the latter without the former. Even dads screw up sometimes.

Brian had always exhibited a sharpness uncommon for his age.

Even a twisted ingenuity seems to have emerged in my little guy. For example: I was living at Hudson St. studios when I was in town working. Every once in a while, I'd take Brian with me for a few days. One day, we walked in to find that the management had installed a new vending machine. It was the kind that the items to be sold were held in a kind of metal corkscrew device, and when the correct number was pushed, the corresponding corkscrew would turn, and the item would fall to the bottom of the machine, where some double trapdoors would allow one to grab the item paid for, without being able to reach up and grab anything else.

Brian looked at this set up for about thirty seconds and said, "Dad, all we have to do is turn the machine upside down with the handtruck, and all the candy will fall off the screws. Pick it back up and all the candy will fall to the bottom where we can get it all free!" I knew then that this industrious little guy was either going to save the world or destroy it. The studio's manager, Juan Carlos, must have overheard us talking because the very next morning two four-by¬fours were affixed from the ceiling to the top of the machine preventing any such machine tipping. My son the safe cracker was foiled.

From the time Brian was old enough to know the difference, every time I went on tour, I brought home a map. On this map, I would outline the route the tour would take in red. While I was away, Brian and China and later my daughter, Marie, would daily trace my progress in blue. The idea was that Daddy wasn't just gone or "on tour" for however long, but he was in a real place called New York or Chicago or Copenhagen. After the midway point of the trip, they could say that I was as far as I was going, and now Dad was heading home, like a great big game of Candyland.

Unbeknownst to me, I had generated an interest in Geography in my son that now enables him to tell you what country I'm pointing at practically anywhere in the world, even if the map has no national indicators. Soon, I'd call home and he would ask something like, "Are you still in Lawrence, Kansas?" or "Are you still in Lincoln, Nebraska?"

When we left San Francisco, heading for our first show in Minneapolis, our van-bus or short bus, which we later named The Blowfish (no relation to Hootie), wasn't ready. We had bought it from the Oakland School District. It used to carry disabled students to grade school, but now was retired to a lot to be sold at a very reasonable price. Nine hundred dollars and she was ours.

Buying from the government is like doing anything else with the government. Red tape makes the simple unbelievably complicated, and that is why the bus we purchased a month earlier wasn't yet cleared by the powers that be. So, due to this unexpected development, we left town in a drive-away car (thanks to Dave's quick-thinking brainstorm). I heard some talk about Brian coming a week or so later with the bus. The bus would be driven by Isha, the wife of Bill (our guitarist at the time), Debbie (our road manager back then), and Tim Armstrong, our roadie and vibes master. Matt, our bass player, and Tim both came from the band Operation Ivy, and went on to form Rancid together.

I had insisted that Brian come with us, as I had promised him and China. So, we started out in our crowded little Ford Taurus on a nonstop cruise east. When we reached the border of Nebraska, I told Brian that knowing what Nebraska looked like on a map is one thing. "Now, my son, you can really see what that little five-inch by three-inch square represents."

It took over eight thunderstorm-filled hours to cross from one end to the other, and a total of over fifty hours to reach our destination and I'm proud to say my four-year-old troubadour did his old man proud. He now also knew the difference between Lincoln, Nebraska and Lawrence, Kansas in terms of time and distance. It took a nonstop day and a half before we pulled into Minneapolis, Minnesota. We arrived early in the morning, and slept until soundcheck.

We were playing a club in Minneapolis where there were a lot of pinball machines. Well, my not deaf, dumb or blind kid can sure play a mean pinball, but after an hour or so on the dollar or so I gave him…
Well, I thought, hey, nobody plays that mean a game of pinball! So I

came up, and after he finished and stepped down off the chair needed to get his little butt high enough to reach the flippers. I watched him. He walked up to a couple, than another... not one minute later, he was in business with half a dozen quarters.

So concerned parent that I am, I asked, "What's the deal, Mr. Pinball?"

Brian told me that he waits for someone at the bar to order two beers. Especially a couple, and notices if they take the eighty-five cents change. He'd already figured out at one dollar plus tax apiece, two beers costs two fifteen. Then he asks the guy for some change for pinball. He also figured out that a guy with a girl was almost a sure thing, since he wouldn't want to appear to be a cheapskate. And with his little smile BINGO! back at the pinball table without missing a beat. I remember thinking that if anyone needs a bridge in Brooklyn or some nice beach front property in Miami... I half-expected to see him roll up his sleeve and sell me a watch. My son was a student of PT Barnum, who said, "There's a sucker born every minute," and WC Fields, who said, "Never give a sucker an even break."

Brian later explained to his square old man that these "nice guys" actually were glad to have the chance to "be a sport" in front of their girlfriends...

"Oh!" I said. "So, in fact, you really were just doing them a favor?" His eyes looked away from me, and he grinned and laughed. We both laughed. It was then that Dave first proclaimed "This not a four-year-old, he'a a midget!"

Shifty "Babyface" Brian's next questionable activity took place, or should I said "was perpetrated at" a bar outside Chicago called Mc-Creedy's. Most states provide for situations involving minors with parents working in bars. Brian would have to steer clear of the bar, but could be around the rest of the building. Some places he would have to stay backstage. A few wouldn't even allow him into their building. Fortunately, most were more reasonable than that.

Anyway, McCreedy's had one of those basketball machines. These machines, upon depositing a coin, lifts a bar that allows miniature basketballs to roll down to where the player can shoot all he can for a certain length of time. Then the bar drops back down, ending the turn. Well, Brian had to stand on the end of the machine in order to shoot. Again, my son is playing for a length of time far beyond his monetary means, and I have to ask myself how. So I watched. Whaddaya know? He's squeezing the balls under the bar. This appeared to be cute and innocent enough. The bartender thought it was a riot. It was, except when Brian confided in me that this was accomplished by taking some of the air out of the balls. The bartender, I'm sure, would have thought differently had he known that my little genius had punctured the balls to get the air out.

There are some things that a dad knows better than a child. One of these is now to deflate a basketball without ruining it. I think McCreedy's barkeep would have lost his sense of humor if he had seen my little menace's skill with a safety pin.

This sort of entertainment for Brian is fine but there would be far more important and valuable lessons to be learned. One inescapable thing to learn is that there are all manners and means of relieving oneself on the road, from someone's private home that they have been gracious enough to allow us to stay, to the gig's bathroom where one might stand at the end of a puddle and piss as close to the toilet or urinal as you can get without wading in, to a tree or garbage can in a back alley behind the bar.

I can happily say that Brian can take of himself in any of these situations. This fact, now having been made public by his thirteenth birthday, will cause his dad more than a word of admonishment. He's also had the thrill of using the famous "hole in the ground with footprints" squat-style Italian toilets. No, it's not just a rumor put forth by other countries competing for the American vacation dollar. However, it should be noted that Italy has plenty of up-to-date facilities for those too squeamish. They did have the very first system that, as Dom DeLuise put it, in the Mel Brooks movie, *History of the World*, "Takes the shit away from your house." You see I love Italy and the Italians too much to want to misrepresent them. (Do you think you can digress a bit more!?) Sorry, Dear Reader.

While we were playing in Chicago, I told our good friend and co-hort, Eric, who was putting us up (or putting up with us) that I wanted to squeeze the Sears Tower and Comiskey Park into the one night we had off. Old Comiskey Park was closing for good that year, and I wanted Brian to see what a real baseball park was like. So we went, and the park was beautiful: big, wooden, square, green, and a real park, as opposed to a stadium. This was the last year the White Sox would be playing there. It was being torn down in favor of an ugly coliseum, stadium-type monstrosity being built right across the street. Who can figure progress?

During the game, I ordered a beer and told Brian to open his mouth and close his eyes. He looked at me funny, but then complied. I quickly spilled some beer into his mouth.

"Yuk," he said. "Why'd ya do that?"

I told him that now he could tell his grandchildren that he had a brew with their great-grandpa Al at old Comiskey Park. I bought him a commemorative grownup-sized t-shirt that read "Comiskey Park, Home of the White Sox 1910-1990" that he still wears proudly.

Later that night — we'd left the game early — we headed downtown. As we approached the Sears Tower on foot at night, it was quite exciting. Twice as exciting for me because I was seeing it up close for the first time, and I was seeing it with my son.

As we approached, we walked under an overhang of the building next door, so we really couldn't see it until we were right across the street from it. Just before we reached the point where we would step out from under the ledge, I told him to stop, take a deep breath, and step out and check out the tallest and biggest building in the world. He did. His eyes got bigger as he looked up and up and up. The Sears Tower is impressive. Kind of a cross between the monolith in *2001: A Space Odyssey* and the Death Star from *Star Wars*: huge, black, and totally massive. We went up to the observation deck and called his mom from seventeen hundred feet in the air. Talk about a view! The night was clear and we could see for miles.

"Guess where we are, Mom?" I could tell by his mom's reaction that she was glad she had let him come.

Meanwhile, it is about two in the morning here in the belly of the beast at Quentin. I'm still locked down 24/7 except for yard, and it's been almost two months. Almost everyone who I arrived with has been shipped to a mainline institution by now. I'm beginning to think that my writing will slow down when they move me to an easy-going ranch, a Community Correction Facility, or some other level one situation. No, they prefer to leave me here in level four, living in Lockdown.

Maybe you're behind this, Dear Reader. Did you pay them to keep me locked in here? Naw, you wouldn't have done that to me, not even for literary reasons. Right?! How about for my own good?

Our itinerary across America eventually found us playing in New York City. I told Brian, "Okay, this is the Big Apple. Everything here is bigger, greater, more fabulous, more scary, deadly. Whatever you name, the best or the worst of it is to be found here. We headed downtown to CBGB where our show was. I warned Brian not to wander around here, it's dangerous! He looked at me with that "I know everything" look, but nodded that he heard and understood.

All of a sudden there's a commotion up at the corner. Some genius was attempting to stiff a taxi driver for a fare, to which the driver was taking exception by beating the man with a chain. The beaten man scampered away bleeding, when we saw what was going on from a safe distance. A crowd had formed to kindly inform the irate hack that his customer had paid enough and to leave him alone. The driver accepted the group's advice, hopped in his cab, and sped off unpaid.

It wasn't ten minutes before we heard the sirens. We thought it was in response to the altercation we had just witnessed, but noooo! Fire trucks whipped around corners from every direction. That same corner where we had just watched the chain-whip spectacle was now center stage for a four-alarm, multi-story fire. The whole building was ablaze; hook and ladders rescuing people from upper floors and everything.

"I told you so, kid," I said. Brian was thrilled.

Brian's call home a half an hour later went something like this:

"Hello?"

"Hi, Mom."

"Hi, dear. Are you in New York yet?"

"Yeah, and boy, is it great."

"Really? Tell me what you're doing."

"Well, we just got here in time to see a man beating up another guy with a chain!"

"WHAT?!"

"Yeah, but the fun didn't really begi until the big fire started."

"I see... LET ME SPEAK TO YOUR FATHER!"

Before we left on tour I explained fully to Brian that there were things I could do for him and things that I couldn't. I could get him to a restaurant for whatever he wanted to eat almost anytime he needed it. Although we rarely like to use them, I could get a hotel whenever we felt it was necessary. I could even reach his mom seventy-five per cent of the time. I couldn't, however, be Mr. Spock and beam him up to his mom or beam her out to us. So he would have to be prepared to be without his mommy for almost two months. I'm glad to say, he never cried for his mommy nor did he ever make any unreasonable demands. He did hit Tim in the head with a softball, but all in all he did great.

I mention these things because Europe was going quite different. Brian handled the States nicely, but in Europe I couldn't promise him all the comforts that homogenized America offers. No Denny's in Villegin-Schwenigen. No Ho-Jo's in Bidgorsch, Poland, and no Motel 6 in Pisa. Telephones are where we find ones we can use. Coin boxes often don't work internationally, and when they do, the language barrier with the operator can be an expensive nightmare. So, realistically, we have to wait until we get to someone's house or business to use a phone. A phone with "clicks" or a counter to measure how much you are spending. Man, those clicks can go by in a hurry, at the equivalent of about thirty-five cents a click, and ten or so clicks a minute, Mommy's voice becomes a luxury. There's also the time differences to consider, like eleven or twelve hours between San Francisco and Moscow.

So, having braved the first tour at four years of age and having had a blast, I might add, at age six with eyes opened wide and armed with all this knowledge about what can and what can't be done in terms of comfort, Brian accompanied his pop on MDC's seventh tour of Europe. This was to be the most extensive tour we would ever undertake. It had us playing many Eastern European countries, including being the first Punk Rock band to play in Russia.

Brian had figured a few things for himself from the first tour. One of these was that he was never going to be wanting for anything. There were, and would be, little surrogate Punk Rock mommies coming out of the woodwork, and people falling over themselves to make sure cute little Mister MDC had anything his little heart desired. His cute, little, manipulative, pouty-faced heart, that is.

He also discovered that if he was going to be involved in a band, he wanted to be the singer. Forget that packing up drums and amplifiers and guitars and stuff. He wanted to step off the stage and belly up to the bar and the girls, just like Uncle Dave! You know, like that band, Dave and the R.oa.d.ies. In all fairness, Dave does, and has always done, his share of roadieing, but it's the nature of a singer to be the center of attention. Of course, Brian loved that.

We now return after the commercial break, Dear Reader, to find that they have finally moved your hero, namely me, to a mainline institution.

So, how does one get moved to the mainline institution once endorsed? (Curious, aren't we?) Well, your day starts as a surprise. Due to the fact that the riskiest part of the whole business of incarceration is the transporting the convicts from one institution to another, secrecy is a priority. This applies to Charles Manson and Night

Stalker Ramirez, for obvious reasons, right on down to a level 4 first termer such as yours truly. The officers on the bus wouldn't want to run into any of my crime syndicate laying an ambush, out to break me out of my chickenshit four or five months of "hard time" at my destination. Who wouldn't jump at the chance to earn five more years for an escape from the ordeal of an air-conditioned little oasis where the guards carry no weapons, a place where no one has more than six months? Consequently, no one is trying to be there one minute longer than necessary. About as peaceful a joint as one could possibly find in the California system.

This, as I have said, makes no difference when you are awakened at 4 a.m. by a guard with a list and a timetable. Thirty minutes later you are marched down to R and R, Receiving and Release.

Now I had been moved to B (Badger) section in South block. B section, you see, is the medical wing of the prison, and conveniently, for me, also was commonly used for overflow convicts. This afforded me the opportunity to stock up with the antidepressant drugs, Elavil, and Melloril. I mention this because at this juncture, I had a healthy supply of each. This, of course, could be an embarrassing little discovery if made by the COs, that would undoubtedly tear my stuff up.

So, what to do with this handful of stress-relieving medication at this time of anxiety? The old six of this and six of that, last-minute gulp trick seemed just the thing, after handing off the rest to my appreciative celly.

My drummer's sense of timing held true because — after the packing, unpacking, being searched, stripped, and furnished with a brand new light blue paper jumpsuit, accessorized as only the California Department of Corrections can, with handcuffs, leg irons, and a belly chain to which said handcuffs were locked — I was feeling less and less pain.

In, fact, by the time the twenty-foot walls and all the barbed wire, razor wire, and sliding chain link fences were giving way to the sights of the free world, I was set to begin a bus ride that, I believe, took between twelve and fifteen hours with a yawn and a nap.

All I remember is awakening at my destination, the Community Correction Facility at Coalinga. I'd like to report that they've found a place that's as hot as the surface of the sun, where no man has gone before. They call this little slice of hell "Coalinga." I know it sounds like a sexual act outlawed in Massachusetts, but in fact it's a little town in central California with a modern little prison. Modern, at least, means air-conditioned. Thank god or Satan for that. This Community Correction Facility, or CCF, is like elementary school. All made of cinderblocks with a courtyard in the middle, but instead of classrooms, there are dorms. The dorms look like a high school gymnasium. There are no bars, just glass and sliding doors that work from the guard booth. The dorms are triangular so that it looks like a giant pizza with the cop booth at the center, so one booth can watch three dorms and the yard at once.

Compared to Quentin, this cute little prison is cake in some ways. Lockdown? There's no place to lock anyone down! They can make you go to your bed and confine you there. Big deal. Everyone here is level one or level two — no violence — just drug offenders and people convicted of other offenses. Levels three and four are the hardened offenders; they get sent to Pelican Bay or old Folsom or Corcoran. That's where you'll find Charlie… Manson! Maximum security.

Patient, virtuous Reader… Dear, dear Reader, my indulgence is nearing an end. And I do miss both my kids terribly. Anyway you'll have to forgive me on this sad June 16, 1996 Father's Day. Now, don't you feel like a heel? We'll both have to "Get over it or die worrying about it," a quote from Buxf Parrot, that bass-playing genius from the The Dicks. (The guy who thought of the name MDC… remember?) Brian decided to accompany his pop on one more tour and had a wonderful time. Even at six years of age he was curious enough and wise enough to have absorbed how different cultures lived and saw many sights he'll never forget. Sights offered to him by his old man. I saved my very favorite Brian story for last.

We were in Poland and staying at the promoter's house. He lived in a tremendous project. Row after row of identically ugly dwellings that were very common in the communist block countries. We get out of the van and there are some kids about Brian's age playing soccer. A few of them came over curious to see who we were. Only one spoke English. He asked if we were from England. Brian said, "No, America!" This excited the kids and soon Brian was playing soccer with them. The following morning Brian got up early and was playing with the same kids. Now in order to keep a six year old occupied on the long drives, I would buy him toys, books, games, anything to help pass the time. So he had a collection of mostly toy cars by the time we reached Poland. Brian had gathered his stuff from the van and was playing at the other end of the field with the other boys. Well it was time to leave and Brian ran over when I called. When he got to the van I saw the other boys were following him with his toys. The kid who spoke English called, "Hey, Brian, you forgot your cars!" Brian looked at me and asked, "Can I leave them here? They don't have much." I told him that would be fine. I knew that he had grown in the time we were gone. I was very proud. In fact, everyone in our crew had seen. And everyone was touched.

Back to the prison town named after an exotic venereal disease, you know, Coalinga. Here in Coalinga the blacks and the Nortenos kick it together, and the peckerwoods and the Surenos kick it together. So the yard and the dorm are ethnically split. In the middle are the pieces, or Mexican Nationals. They don't kick it with either group. The whole thing is like living in an Ice-T movie or Sean Penn, perhaps; a cross between *Colors* and *Bad Boys*. In any case, although it's level one there's still an uncomfortably tight situation in which one watches one's back always. No security of a locked cell to keep you safe.

As in Quentin, people take their racism very seriously. Though everyone relates to one another as convicts, the groups allow each other enough space and respect that sworn enemies will demand or else "IT'S ON!" My being relatively small compared to most of these weight-pit thugs, and being white in the minority, I tread softly and keep to myself. While I haven't seen any trouble yet here in Coalinga, the potential of the mixed dorm to become a huge race riot is obvious. This potential and its propensity for escalation greatened by the lack of preparedness by the guards. No gun towers or catwalks and NO GUNS! Any OG status won't be counting for exemption should the shit hit the fan! At one point, there was only one wood and one Sureno in the dorm or pod, as the others had done their fish time and were transferred to their permanent dorms. Fortunately, the next day found a new group of fish arriving containing four or five woods so the balance is better or safer now.

Upon introducing myself to the new 'woods, one of them called me "Big Al." I told him the story of how, when I was in the county jail in San Bruno, I had the big bag of commissary. Another fellow in the San Bruno who had the big sack weekly was Tracy H. He used to make a "spread" every night. A spread is where you take a couple (as many as possible) of soup ramens like generic cup noodles from people who wanted to be in on the spread, add meat saved from lunch, dinner vegetables from dinner, and some hot spicy pork rinds or Texas-style hot potato chips, and put them all into a new garbage bag. Add boiling water, and there you go! The perfect before bed snack.

To get in on the spread, you kick in a soup and some of the aforementioned ingredients. Your percentage of the spread would always be much greater and much tastier than if you ate the soup alone. There would always be enough to feed an extra person or two of Tracy's choosing, a privilege given him 'cause he was the one who collected up and made the spread.

When Tracy got TXed out, he left me his seat at the head of the 'woods table. He also left me in charge of running the spread. He also left me the name "Big Al," because of my Santa (or Jed Clampett) sack.

One day, some fish arrive at Bruno. It's around dinnertime and one of the fish innocently sits down in my seat. Someone informed him that he was sitting in Big Al's chair and that he had better move. He quickly got up, apologizing, and said that he didn't know. A few minutes later, I was sitting in my seat just before dinner, and this same guy who had made the faux pas in the seating arrangement earlier tells me that I'd better get up. I replied, "Oh, yeah? Why?" The answer, which I already knew, came, …because I was in Big Al's seat.

I told him, "Well, you go tell Big fuckin' Al that if he's got a problem, to come over and kiss my ass."

He smiled and said, "Okay, guy," and walked off in anticipation of getting to see some skinny, big mouth, wiseguy get in a wreck with Big Al. I sat back and watched his shit-eating grin drop upon finding out that I was Big Al! That's right, BIG FUCKING AL!

Well, big on having a sack befitting a DRUG LORD. That's right again; the boys inside decided I was Big Al, and the cops decided I was a drug lord. I'm happy to say that I think I was big of heart in a fairly heartless trade. And if someone (like the pigs) want to call me a Lord… yeah, well, compared to them — worms and vermin that they are — well, I surely won't argue the status as Lord. Shhhh, I know I'm not God (I think, probably not) but don't tell the cops…

26

Coalinga only lasted a few months for me as I quickly became eligible for work furlough. This was July or August 1996. A week of lock-in at the Indiana Street Work Furlough house, and I sought and got a job as a bicycle messenger. It was a job that I could deal with. Give me a radio and send me on my way. No indoor job for me. I'd had enough of the great indoors.

A few months later, and I was free except for parole. During these work furlough months I'd managed to stay straight. Being UAed (subjected to urine analysis) every couple of days did the trick. I held myself in check by reminding myself that no matter how much I love drugs, I hated prison even more.

On the subject of parole: it seems that California has a big money problem. For the first time in history, this state's correction officers and deputies' unions are bigger than the teachers' union. In fact, the business of incarceration is the number one industry in California. They want to place 6,000 more people, mostly men, in prison by the end of the century. Most of these will be parole violators. The state receives $3300 for each inmate from the federal government. After I heard some of the trumped-up bullshit the cops were using to have an excuse to shakedown people on parole, I decided to move away.

A friend of mine, Tommy, was visited by the cops for supposedly running guns with or for the Hell's Angels. I know Tom, and I know the Angels, and I know bullshit when I hear it. With nothing really to keep me there, I decided to move north to Portland. The guitarist before Bill, Eric Calhoun, lived in Portland, Oregon. He had moved here to be with his wife, Jenny Joe, who was also Dave's ex and the mother of Dave's son, Jesse. So when I went in, not only did my kids and China move nearer to her mother in McKinleyville, California, but Dave moved up to Portland to be closer his son. All these factors made San Francisco less of a necessary place to be.

So, newly released from furlough, and not eager to financially aid the great state of California, I moved north. North to Portland. I figured I wouldn't be as tempted to run guns, or whatever the excuse du jour they would manufacture for me. The fact is that parolees are subject to searches without warrants or even probable cause, so any excuse will hold water if you don't need one to begin with.

I heard the figure ninety percent referring to the number of parolees that would do at least one violation. Of those, eighty-five percent would do more than one.

"If you can't find Justice, it will find YOU!" Gary Floyd sings in the song "Dicks Hate the Police." The hope was, and is, that "justice" would have a far more difficult time finding me here.

MDC would play just three shows with a line-up consisting of Eric (who played with MDC for a couple of years and recorded *Metal Devil Cokes* with us) on guitar, and Joe from Speed Racer on bass. We ended appropriately on a high note playing with Ice T's Body Count He said we were original cop killers. While that may not be true, it's the thought that counts and coming from Ice T… well, we'll take the compliment.

After that, Dave and I just continued as friends. We remain that way today. In many ways, it's much nicer not to have all that pressure on our friendship. No heartfelt differences of opinion. Of course, the downside is that sometimes we sorely miss performing. We sure did love to play and make music.

As for my darker profession, I still tried to do the same thing, just far more cautiously. I would think of everything I do as if I were re-thinking it through in the holding tank. Like, "What the fuck was I doing in that loud car with stuff on me? You must've been out of your fucking mind!" or "What was I going to make on this or that deal? Was it worth it?" Just trying to head off the stupidity before it heads me off to prison with an enhancement for having a prison prior. But things had changed and I just wasn't that guy anymore.

I also try to remember that anyone who would have you do something that puts you at risk, or even have you do something that you don't want to do, this person cannot be considered a friend, not really. It's more of the Politics of a Front.

The front, you ask, Dear Reader? Well, the front's an allegory both for the high time spent for two and a half years. The payback was aching for the things I had learned to take for granted. Things like the simple ability to look up at the sky whenever I wanted to or eating the foods I wished when I wished them. These privileges denied me in prison came to have new meaning. I remember having my first sip of Pepsi in five months. Until that second I had no idea how much I missed that taste, that burn in my throat. It actually tasted as if it had rum in it. These are small things.

The greater things are more obvious. The hug of my daughter or her high-pitched, excited voice at hearing that it was her daddy on the phone. Christ, the smell of women is so sweet. God, when I first got out and hugged Clarissa and Mayginn and Catherine I knew what the romanticists meant. Their voices are music, and the air around them vibrates with a smell of life so vital, so clear that without its vibration, I'd just as soon jump off the Golden Gate Bridge. I knew eventually the nightmares I would be able to know were just that, even as they were happening, instead of just being part of my whole existence. I mentioned before how I'd dream the cops were after me, and when I woke the real nightmare was realizing that they caught me. Then, of course, my freedom was a high price.

I'd have to come in head-to-head disagreement with Kris Kristofferson, or at least where his lyric claims that "Freedom's just another word for nothing left to lose." Surely, having lost mine for a while made me keenly aware of everything else I did have to lose.

"Nothing ain't worth nothing, but it's free..." Yes, perhaps, Kris, but I suggest that to be "free" of having to worry about the welfare of loved ones who depend on you, this isn't worth "nothing," it's worth everything.

"My kingdom for a horse," or my big toe for one night to be home in the middle of my term, or the chance to wipe my little girl's cheek free of tears the next time some small but serious sadness fills her. Forgive my semantics, Kris. I meant no disrespect. After all, anyone who would "trade all his tomorrows for a single yesterday" is surely as incurable a romantic as I.

Well, I remain grasping for answers and unsure of the questions. Up to this point I've been a college student, a prep cook, a real estate agent, an equipment manager, recording artist, a traveling entertainer (or so say our working papers, when applicable), a decoy for a grocery store shoplifting conspiracy, songwriter, drummer (you know, "1, 2, 3, 4"), Punk Rock ambassador both here and especially abroad, and a good listener — a skill acquired by tiring of the sound of one's own voice, and from flagrantly exercising my right to be dead wrong. Let me say, more incomplete than wrong; sometimes it's the same thing, sometimes not. I, furthermore, have seen myself grow from being rather judgmental to deciding that mine was not to judge, even if I was willing to be judged.

On the other side — the dark side, if you please — I made an excellent criminal. We all may have differing definitions of crime. I, for example, provided a service, one greatly in demand with which I could barely keep up. I watched myself go from sniffing around for the money for quarter-grams to moving quarter-pounds on a weekly basis. I was making good money, and I thought I could buy myself out of any legal difficulty I got myself into. This, my friends, was not the case. With traps like "the three-year joint suspended," and any other sleazy deals the courts in California have cooked up to clear their dockets, they set you up like (as Garcia, RIP, often sang) a bowling pin. And they play the waiting game. Then they put on the pressure and watch you fall. No expensive trial necessary! He's already pleaded guilty when he took the deal! All the courts need do is revoke the "privilege" of probation, and reinstate your pen time.

In conclusion, except for my newfound passion for reading and my newly discovered ability to write, you might say that the whole experience left me right back where I started. This I couldn't deny.

"If I knew then, what I know now, do you think I would have been so blind?" So asks Procol Harum's singer Gary Brooker.

Well, as for me, probably not... but maybe so. That is, while there are regrets I have, especially with my mother and children whom my going to prison taxed so harshly, and prison itself I obviously would have avoided, if possible. But I won't apologize for my dealing and I loved being the big shot, the guy with the cash. I liked my little orange sportscar and my BMW motorcycles, my fancy jewelry. I DO realize that all those things could have been acquired legally and at far less cost to my friends and loved ones. And while I used to say "we are all big boys and girls," referring to the people who bought my wares, and being fully aware that they would make their purchases elsewhere if not from me. I still feel badly for those I caused any harm. So, I wouldn't say that I haven't learned anything and that I would gladly pay the consequences to have it all over again. No, that was then, and this is now. I was a good convict and learned a different reality. Such changes are very seldom invited, and any benefits have to be strained and strived for. I know how sweet freedom is and fear that someday I will have to square up with the CDC. I'm not looking forward to that day, but will I whine? Fuck no! I wouldn't give those fucking COs the satisfaction. I am, after all, an original member of MDC.

However, allow me to peel back a layer or two of self-serving aggrandizing, and plainly and clearly proclaim that I was always aware that what I was involved in had unseen victims. For those folks, again, I am sorry, and as for the nice things I was able to do, it could have been achieved without breaking the law. And the stuff I kept (or tried to keep), I could have easily done without. Hey, Reader, just keeping it real. Truthfully, I do have considerable amounts of regret and remorse. That's where a bit of time, and hopefully wisdom, has since shaped my memory and attitude towards others.

And so as I sink in the western sun or walk away or fade to black, I ask not deference or pity, nor do I cry the blues, for it is enough for me to know that I've earned the right to. Besides I've a new endeavor. And it's a self-fulfilling prophecy told by the fact that you are sharing this moment with me. Since you are, then I can assume that my effort has been a success. My new endeavor, you ask? Well, I was thinking of becoming an author.

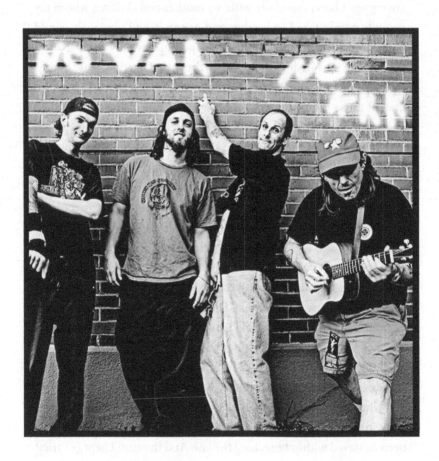

EPILOGUE

More than twenty years have passed since pen was put to paper in the writing of this book. Dave and I finally wound up continuing doing what we were always meant to do: make music and travel the country and world in order to share it.

We now share 15 albums and have traveled all over. We played Asia this year: China, Indonesia, Malaysia, Singapore, Thailand, and Japan. I was along on 16 of MDC's 21 European tours, and we are still going strong.

Now in my seventh decade, I'm thankful for every damn day and go out of my way to keep all the "strokes" on the drums. The way we have aged as a band is like fine wine. The current government has given us renewed energy for being the angry young men we were; we are just not young anymore. Our song "Born to Die" has been picked up anew by protesters: "No Trump! No KKK! No Fascist USA!"

Dave and I both wrote books. We live in Portland. My son Brian has grown up to be a successful businessman doing something he loves, and lives nearby. We are still very close. What more could a father ask for?

All and all, I would have to say that life is good.

ACKNOWLEDGMENTS

Thanks to the photographers and flyer artists whose work appears in these pages. If your work appears uncredited within, please accept our apologies and contact us so that we may update this info.

Back cover author photo: Jessica Mitchell

Photo by Ed Colver: pp 4

Photo by Selena: pp 136

Photos by Rhoda Rohnstock: pp 2, 50, 80, 104, 124

Photo by Candace Blakenship/*Maximum RocknRoll*: pp143

The author and publisher offer sincere gratitude to Dave Dictor and Ron Posner for their assistance and support in producing this book.

Disclaimer: This book is a memoir, a narrative composed from memories of personal moments as best as the author can remember experiencing them. Apologies if you remember things differently or if the author has gotten names, dates, places, or anything else wrong.